MW01015942

About the Author

DeRay Williams has enjoyed a successful career as a Spinal Cord Injury, Intensive Care and Emergency Room Nurse in Seattle, WA area for many years. As a Nursing Supervisor, DeRay is driven by his passion and commitment to help others in need. He is a husband, father and a grandfather.

He has always made God and his family his first priorities in life.

Dedication

To Walter H. Williams (Zanagi Rasool) who passed away in his sleep on 4th March 2015. My brother Walter was a true hero to many people, as a Boxer, Police Officer and a Postal Employee. He dedicated his life in helping others, and supporting many family members.
May God rest his soul in peace, Walter will be deeply missed.

DeRay Williams

THREE STRIKES
YOU'RE OUT

AUSTIN MACAULEY
PUBLISHERS LTD.

A CIP catalogue record for this title is available from the British Library.

ISBN 9781785542442 (Paperback)
ISBN 9781785542459 (Hardback)
ISBN 9781785542466 (E-Book)

www.austinmacauley.com

First Published (2016)
Austin Macauley Publishers Ltd.
25 Canada Square
Canary Wharf
London
E14 5LQ

Acknowledgments

Three Strikes was written to inspire and unify Americans to a common goal, the health and welfare of our nation, united we stand and divided we fall. For our Afro-American ancestors, institutionally and systematically robbed of their basic human rights. Rights guaranteed by the United States Constitution; rights of freedom, life liberty and the pursuit of happiness. Their dreams were that someday the playing fields of America will be even, there will be a Black President of the United States.

I want to thank my beautiful wife Susan Schnarr-Williams, my mother Frances L. Williams, and my entire extended family in the United States and Canada, for all their support and encouragement while writing this book.

I also want to thank my friends and co-workers for their thoughts and comments on certain aspects of this book.

Table of Contents

Preface   13
Introduction   17
Chapter 1   29
The paradigm to baseball   29
Chapter 2   35
Privileged and non-privileged groups in America   35
Chapter 3   40
Strong Religious Background   40
Chapter 4   44
Living in Fear   44
Chapter 5   50
Separate but equal   50
Chapter 6   54
Systematic discrimination   54
Chapter 7   60
Growing up in the South   60
Chapter 8   70
Growing up in the North   70
Chapter 9   82
Seattle Washington   82
Chapter 10   85
Discrimination continues   85
Chapter 11   90
U.S. Presidents, Slavery and Civil Rights   90
Chapter 12   100
The First Black American President   100
Chapter 13   109
Even the baseball field   109
Chapter 14   114
Comments from family and friends   114
Summary   119
Bibliography   125

Preface

In the beginning, God created the Heavens and Earths, and God created men and women of all walks of life equal, regardless of biological, social or ethnic orientation. America is God's land, and The Church is its foundation, the centrepiece that holds this great nation together, the solid rock.

As rational human beings, we all know right from wrong, what should be and what should not be; yet we continue to let bad laws and policies of special interest groups hinder our growth as a nation. Blacks, women, and all non-white Americans were not allowed voting rights in one unforgettable dark period of our nation's history; why? Special interest groups wanted control and power.

Three Strikes laws of the 1980's were intended to be tough on crime, take violent repeat offenders off the street. Three strike laws continue to put many young black men, minorities and poor people in prison for petty crimes; why? Because they could not afford attorneys to plea bargain; a public defender just wants a speedy trial, to clear his case load. Stand Your Ground laws were intended to protect innocent people, self-defence was the claim in many cases; yet it put many young, innocent black youths at risk of being murdered because they look suspicious; some as young as nine years old. Over 25 children and teens have been murdered in Florida alone, using Stand Your Ground laws as their defence.

Trayvon Martin, not yet 18 years old, walking home from his neighbourhood store with just candy and a soda, no gun; was followed by a vigilante and murdered for looking suspicious. 17 year old Jordan Davis and two other teens were opened fire upon at a corner store in their neighbourhood for not turning down the music on their car radio. Would those 40 year old vigilantes have shot white kids? As Americans, our primary goal in life should be making life better for ourselves and others; protecting our children; we are our brother's keepers. Together we should share the many glories, possibilities, and wonders this great nation has to offer. We have pledged our allegiance to the flag; one nation under God, indivisible, with liberty and justice for all; especially children. The Supreme Court is sworn to serve and protect; they should protect young, innocent children. State sovereignty should not be put in front of the right to live. For God's sake, our leaders should work together to reverse discriminatory laws that target specific groups in America.

Sit back and relax, and enjoy a good book, one that everyone can enjoy and benefit from reading. *Three Strikes* is a true story, based on actual facts, no names have been changed. *Three Strikes* is entertaining from start to finish; it will take you on an up and down emotional journey, inspire your faith in God and humanity, and conclude with a happy ending.

Like the game of baseball, each batter is supposed to have three strikes at bat; but like my grandfather and many other grandfathers of the past has always said, "you only get one strike at bat if you are black, just because of the colour of your skin". The analogy to baseball is that each strike represents a civil liberty for black people. Strike one represents equal opportunity (no jobs), strike two represents equal protection (No lynching), and strike three represents equal representation under the law (no black officials); which was finally obtained with the election of the first

Black President of the United States. Now black people in America can finally have their full three strikes at bat.

Three Strikes was written to inspire and unify Americans to a common goal, the health and welfare of our nation; united we stand and divided we fall. The enemy lurking in our own back yard is greed and profit-motivated special interest groups, with no concern for the health and welfare of our nation. Their only motivation is personal gains, at the expense on anyone who gets in their way.

Since the days of slavery, special interest groups in America and abroad were busy at work, fighting hard to keep the slave trade industry alive, so the self-interest profit motivated groups of people can make profits off the sweat and hard, cheap labour of slaves. They had no concern for humanity, yet most slave owners called themselves god fearing Americans who live in the land of the free.

Special interest groups fought to the bitter end against voting rights legislation for women and minorities in America, their fears were that power and control will be taken away from them. Today special interest groups are fighting against healthcare and marijuana reforms; they don't want Americans to have free healthcare, or better pain control, they want to make a profit, and raise the cost. Americans should not keep damaging their health on harmful products like cigarettes, drugs and alcohol, and then be forced to pay inflated health insurance costs. Many Americans are shortening their life expectancy because they can't afford healthcare coverage. Just having a physical once every year can provide early detection for many curable diseases, which could otherwise have been fatal.

Special interest groups support the existence of discrimination in America today; they want affirmative action laws repealed; private companies would not have to hire a certain number of minorities and women. Do you think that is right for America? We live in a multicultural land of the free; a land where no one should be denied justice or equal opportunity. If you are unaware of the huge employment disparities in America, this book will help clear up some of your misconceptions.

Introduction

I can remember growing up in the Deep South in the early 1950's, well, as deep in the south that I have ever been for any period of time, Fordyce, Arkansas. I visited Raleigh, North Carolina, Kentucky and Kansas for brief periods, but never lived there. As a young child growing up in Fordyce, Arkansas, our house looked pretty big to me. It was one of the bigger homes on the block. Most of the homes in our neighbourhood were small, cylinder block row homes built for the nearby saw mill workers and their families. I can remember using an outhouse, because there were no indoor toilets in the black community at that time. Most of the people in the black community were still using an outside man-made well to get drinking water. Hot water had to be heated on a wood burning stove, and then poured into a tin bath tub to take a bath. When the bath was done, the water was carried outside by two kids, and dumped. The younger kids had to use the same bath water twice, because filling up the tub was no easy task.

My grandfather's father was an ex-slave, brought to the United States on a slave ship from the West Indies. His father was just a child when he was separated from his two brothers by slave traders; sold to plantation owners, and never saw his brothers again, for over 40 years. My grandfather Columbus Thrower was tall, over six feet, a strong, dark skinned black man; married to Ella Lee Thrower, a very beautiful part Indian woman, with green eyes and long, wavy dark hair. Mom said we have some relatives in Ohio and Kansas somewhere; but we are not exactly sure where.

My grandmother's mother was part Blackfoot American Indian; her family was there long before the settlers arrived. Ella loved the outdoors. She was a hard-working woman, always working in the yard; which includes the garden, cornfield or doing laundry. To do the laundry she had to boil clothes in a big, black pot, with fire burning under it, add lye soap and stir, scrub the delicate clothes on a scrub board, rinse, then hang them out to dry on an outdoor line. She had seven children and a husband to clean and cook for, seems like she was always doing laundry.

Grandfather wanted his children and grandchildren to be self-sufficient. He taught us how to farm, hunt and fish, and he always saw to it that there were plenty of vegetables, beans, potatoes, fish, chicken, rabbit, beef and pork to eat. Every morning we would have eggs or grits, and every Sunday we would have chicken, mashed potatoes and gravy after returning from church. Grandpa was a deacon, grandma sung in the choir, and everyone went to church.

The small town that I grew up in, part of my childhood life, was called Fordyce; just 90 miles from the big city of Littlerock, Arkansas. Typical of small towns in the state, you can stand at one end of the main section of uptown and see the other end; there was one bank, one post office, and one drug store. People often said that if you were traveling on a bus and closed your eyes for a second, you would miss the whole town. Fordyce was a beautiful country town in the spring time, lots of tall, green trees everywhere, dirt roads and railroad tracks. People usually could tell the time of the day by the freight and passenger trains that pass on schedule through the small town. I could remember sleeping real good at night, hearing the rain drop on a nearby tin roof, and that old Rock Island Express blowing in the distance.

My grandfather's home was on one side of the tracks, my grandmother's sister, Ivory Steele, had a home across the street, and my grandfather's son, who is my uncle, L.G. Thrower, had a home on the other side of the tracks. This was an all-black section of town. The town was segregated into all black and all white sections, and the whites always had the better sections; the whites did not want to be close to the loud trains going by every day. As kids, we often played games on the tracks. Those were fun times, games like skip the log tiles, who could balance on one rail the longest as we walked to visit relatives, going to school, church, up town or the grocery store. Columbus and Ella Lee Thrower raised seven children, five girls and two boys. Ella's maiden name was Steele; she had a sister and brother, named Ivory and Toot, and they also had a large family, which made up the rest of the Thrower-Steele family living in Fordyce, Arkansas.

Many older adults can remember from history classes about the famous Littlerock Nine: in 1957, the governor of Arkansas, Orville Faubus, defied a federal order to integrate public schools in Littlerock, the capital of Arkansas. Governor Faubus called up the National Guards to block the integration of nine black students from starting school at Little Rocks Central High School. President Dwight D Eisenhower had to send Federal Troops to the school to enforce integration and support the students. You can still read about this on the internet. Like most of the small towns in Arkansas during the 1950's, Fordyce was outside of the federal spotlight and media attention, therefore they did what they wanted. They did not integrate all the schools; some of those small rural southern schools are still segregated today.

Most black people in that small town were quiet, withdrawn, complacent, and kept in line by fear, afraid of white intimidations and threats. Stories were often told about black male disappearances and lynching, black women being raped, Jim Crow laws and hate organizations like the KKK. Blacks were systematically denied land ownership, physically robbed of personal properties and land they legally owned. I personally had the opportunity, as a black registered nurse, to interview several black males on their death beds, and they wanted to vent their frustrations on past injustices towards black people. Their stories were about their parents and relatives, who were mistreated, denied ownership of deeds to land legally signed over by plantation owners to them upon their death, but mysteriously the deeds and land transfers were lost, and the land was given to the city, and then sold to the highest bidder.

Blacks were institutionally denied equal education in the south, the schools were sub-standard, books were used, donated from local all-white segregated schools, last year's books. To no surprise there was no black history, just history classes; because most of the accomplishments by blacks in the early days were credited to white people; all the drawings and pictures depicted on the pages of the books were white people.

Through all their adversities, black people had a strong faith in God; they prayed that someday a change would come. My mother, Francis L. Williams of Denver, Colorado, felt strongly about a change coming, she often stated that, "change is coming for the salvation of all mankind. It's not completely here yet, but it is coming." My mother's belief was that all children should go to church and Sunday school. She thought that children need a strong religious background to provide options and direction when facing life's challenges. When you are raised in a strong religious environment, you don't stray too far in life from goodness and truth. Black people must be strong, stay focused, cut out all the youth violence, gang activity and drive-by shootings; kids should go back to the days of church activities, which played a big part in keeping kids off the street and out of trouble with the law. All children need a family support system, black adolescent boys especially need a positive male leadership image, like a father figure, whether an uncle, grandfather, or cousin, to help mothers teach young adolescents right from wrong, and provide alternative resources to channel their energy and aggression.

A lot of the mistreatment of blacks in slavery times, like house burnings and lynchings by out of control mobs, were instigated by hate groups like the KKK, who preyed on the fears of people with lies and deceit; they spread false rumours about Blacks, like that they had tails and smaller brains. Older folks use to tell stories about how some young white kids thought it was true. People could see that some blacks were physically stronger; that is because most blacks preformed the heavy labour and worked the fields as slaves. Genetics also played a part as they were bred to be big, strong and fast. It makes sense that some blacks could probably excel in certain areas that require physical conditioning, such as Mohamed Ali, Michael Jordan, Tiger Woods, Venus and Serena Williams; they dominate sports that were off limits to blacks 50 years ago. These are perfect examples of how blacks have overcome major challenges in life.

Blacks are good with humour; they use laughter, dance and religion to ease their pain. They could sing, dance, and had good athletic ability because of years of conditioning. When you hear Redd Foxx, Richard Pryor, James Brown and Michael Jackson, understand that they inherited their skills from their parents, who inherited their skills from their parents; slaves would work hard, sing, dance, and tell jokes to keep their sanity. We, "The United States of America", still have a long way to go as a nation as we strive to be true humanitarians like many other countries.

We must learn to respect people for who they are, not what they are.

We, as Americans, must address the roots of racial disparities in America. People are not so much the problem today, but the discriminatory laws, policies and customs of the past, like filibuster and the two thirds majority rule, which gives power to the minority and special interest groups in a democracy, where the majority should rule.

Political handcuffs in congress, which block legislation of laws desperately needed for the prosperity and benefit of all America, have created a foundation for racial disparities in healthcare, employment, and housing. The Supreme Court should actively seek out and appeal discriminatory laws on the federal, state and local levels. There are people who believe that not all Americans are entitled to quality health care, and we should do away with affirmative action and racial hiring quotas. But I say they are absolutely wrong; healthcare is a humanitarian issue, and should not be a political issue. We all should have coverage, and should demand free National Healthcare. Without employment quotas and affirmative action, the systematic discrimination against women and minorities of yesterday will continue to grow; like roots embedded underground of a tree, cut off the top and it will continue to grow. Eventually we must get down to the roots of America's problems; greed, self-centred small groups of individuals seeking wealth, control, and power.

We are all brothers and sisters in the eyes of God; sibling rivalry has been going on since the biblical days of Cain and Abel, the two sons of Adam and Eve. One brother was jealous of the other, so he murdered him; when asked where his brother is, he replies, "Am I my brother's keeper?" Yes, we are our brothers' keepers, and what is done in darkness will someday be seen in the light.

Between 1950 and 1960, Dick Clark made millions with American Bandstand, featuring black entertainers like

Donna Summers and Michael Jackson; Elvis Presley made millions dancing like Jackie Wilson and singing like Fats Domino, the group Average White Band and Slim Shady sold a lot of records singing black music and rapping. In 1971 Soul Train became the longest running syndicated program in history, but did not make Don Cornelius as wealthy as Dick Clark. Why? Because the television and radio producers and owners paid less to black entertainers; they showed what they wanted to see and hear on television and radio. Today there are still very few black television and radio station producers and owners in America.

Take a look at the movie industry. Everyone knows that in the past, the black man was always the first to die in an action movie, unless he or she is the main character; they were just racial quotas forced on the movie industry. The movie industry is also similar to baseball in a paradigm of the black man's struggle for equality; it has been customary that blacks were the last to be hired, and the first to go when layoffs come. Why? Because they are black and have one strike against them already.

With the election of a black President in 2008, we start to notice a change in Hollywood. We see more blacks in commercials and leading roles on television shows and movies; most of these shows, movies and commercials with blacks are not new productions, but just now being released to air because the industry feels the change coming; they are propelled to show more blacks in a favourable, modern image. Don't be fooled by what you see on television or the local media, television is forced by affirmative action and quotas to show a percentage of minorities in the media, but in real life, blacks are still the minority. Black Americans continue to have a much lower percentage of politicians, movie producers, business CEO's, sports franchise owners, book publishing company and private business ownerships than white Americans.

Please don't get me wrong, I am not prejudice against any group of people; one of my best friends growing up, David Hilliard from Southern California, is white, and another friend, Philbert Montoya of Denver, Colorado is Hispanic. Throughout my entire life, I have been taught to treat everyone equally, especially as an ACLS Registered Nurse. I respect the rights of others and treat all gods' people with respect and dignity, regardless of race or nationality. My grandparents and parents were always very religious, they believed that god has an ultimate plan for love, peace and unity on earth. God's ultimate plan will prevail on earth, and will not be prevented by groups of people motivated by self-interest, greed, profit or power.

My current wife, Susan Schnarr-Williams, my mother- and father-in-law, and my sisters- and brothers-in-laws, are white Canadian. We have a large, energetic and happy family, and we all get along well. We don't see race as an issue. Social standing outside the United States plays a significant role in race relations. Susan has a very prominent and influential family on the Canadian side of the border. Susan's father, Vern Schnarr, is self-employed and retired from BF Goodrich; his wife Yvonne is the leader of the group, the alpha-female, she keeps the house in order, and is a very sweet, kind, wonderful person, active in planning most of the family events. Sue's brother Mark Schnarr carried the 2010 Winter Olympic Torch through parts of Canada; he is a business and community leader, President and CEO of a communications firm. Susan's sister, Jill Schnarr, is a community leader and Vice President of Community Affairs for Telus Communications; she introduced Hilary Rodham Clinton at a recent Board of Trade event in Canada on March 5, 2014. Her other brother, Perry Schnarr, is a Captain for the fire department, and active community leader; Gwen, Gaye, and Janie have great jobs and outstanding careers. The list goes on, Don, Rita, Laurie, Craig, Tom and Dave, all beautiful people. The entire family played a big part in the completion of this book, they were the typical non-American family, unaware of the many injustices to minorities in the United States, their interest and curiosity in this book deeply encouraged me to write. They were all jumping for joy and partying in the streets all over British Columbia in 2010 when Canada won the Gold Medal in Ice Hockey, they beat the United States 3 to 2. The crowds were wild, like the Fourth of July, the party was on.

Stephen Harper and the rest of the House of Commons should be very proud of the Canadian Hockey Team's accomplishments, and the fans for great sportsmanship. The Canadians were humble in victory, giving the Americans praise for a gallant effort. Canada did an outstanding overall job in the 2010 Winter Olympics in Vancouver, B.C; hats off to all the athletes and sponsors, they were perfect host to the world. Canada showed the world that they have the resources to put on one of the best winter Olympics ever; the city was beautiful, they were prepared, everything was in place.

The Olympic Games was a huge boost to the local economy, the world got to see how beautiful Canada was, the real estate sales and prices in certain areas were on the rise. Canada deserved to win the gold medal in ice hockey, they wanted the victory the most, they were playing at home in front of all their fans, they could not lose. Hockey is one of their National games; they have been playing it longer than Americans. If Canada played the United States in basketball or football, depending on where they played, and fan support, America would more than likely win.

You can read all about the phenomena of victory and competition in my second book, "Black Reign, The African American Athlete" not released yet. The team or players who have the most drive, determination and motivation to win, will win. Support from fans and spectators, like the 12th man in football, help influence the outcome of the games. Part of our humanity is that we all want to see people do better, and the fans in most situations always support their home team or the underdog.

Vancouver and Seattle support each other in sports, regardless of the race of the players. In 2014 Sochi Winter Olympics, Canada won the men's and women's gold medals in hockey again, the celebrations were on, and they love their sports. There were huge celebrations all over Vancouver when the Seattle Seahawks won the Super Bowl in 2014, the sports fans in Vancouver are strong supporters of the Seattle Seahawks and the Seattle Mariners baseball team.

Disparities in race relations is mostly an American phenomenon, because slavery on a mass market did not exist after the 17th century in any other country; racial disparities declined in all other countries. The British Parliament and African Sultans of 1840-1876 closed the slave trade from Africa, but illegal slave trading still went on for many years. Many countries abandoned their slave practices, because of interracial marriages, and mixed raced children. Southern states made interracial marriages illegal for many years, and southern attitudes were that if a person had one drop of African blood in their family, they are considered second class citizens.

If the greatest nation on this earth, America would have refused to accept the slaves brought over on the ships commissioned by other countries like Britain, France and Spain for profit, racial discrimination and healthcare disparities would be obsolete in America today. Greed and profit led slave hunters to Africa and caused African tribes of yesterday to wage war on other tribes just to sell their prisoners to the slave traders heading to America. Why did America accept slaves in the first place? One reason is that America was a new nation with no true leaders or system of government; the colonies from England and France needed the cheap labourers to cultivate the new land.

Let's make it perfectly clear that throughout the Black struggle in America, there have been many white Americans, mostly northerners, who stood up against slavery, racial prejudices and discrimination. Abraham Lincoln stood up against slavery; Harry S. Truman and Dwight D. Eisenhower stood up for integration, and John F. Kennedy stood up for Civil Rights. First Ladies Eleanor Roosevelt and Hillary Rodham Clinton stood up for black people. Eleanor wanted equal opportunity for blacks, and Hillary, during her husband's presidential administration between 1993 and 2001, helped many black children with her State Children's Health Insurance Programs, which increased healthcare coverage for low income families; she wrote the book, *It Takes a Village*. Hillary advocated for Universal Healthcare, women's rights, equal pay for women, breast cancer research, and teenage pregnancy, and she fought the big drug companies for better safety regulations. Many other freedom organizations had a large number of White Americans working for the cause of liberating black people from slavery, like the Underground Railroad. We all remember from history classes the important roles of Harriet Tubman and Frederick Douglas in the Underground Railroads. There were also white Americans like Susan B. Anthony, one of the founders of the women's suffrage movement, whose face is on our U.S. silver dollar, Allan Pinkerton of the famous Pinkerton Detective Agency, and many other white people who risked their lives by providing food, shelter and financial support for the fugitive slaves escaping to the north.

The great American melting pot theories of the 18th Century are still alive and well today. We live in a multicultural, multi-nationality country. We have more different nationalities than any other country in the world. We have entire communities, neighbourhoods and shopping districts of African, Asian, Chinese, Russian and other influences. Interracial marriages are legal in every state in

America, and we have children and young adults today who do not choose to be labelled by a certain distinct nationality or race, they just consider themselves as American.

We need free healthcare for all children and low income families in America. Where is our humanity? We should want to see people do better. We need more community-based hospitals and free health clinics in our neighbourhoods than banks and credit unions. We need more minority state and federal government officials and black private business owners in America to step up to the plate and be proactive in implementing policies to improve employment opportunities for minorities. We still need affirmative action and race quotas in employment hiring policies to balance the scales of past racial inequities, and to improve the quality of life for all America.

Chapter 1

The Paradigm to Baseball

My grandfather, Columbus Thrower, son of an ex-slave brought to the U.S. from the West Indies on a slave ship, was a huge fan of baseball; he always listened to baseball on the radio, or watched baseball on television when it became available. The first baseball games were televised in the early 1940's, but television was not available to most of the black community until the early 1950's. In the beginning days of baseball, there were few black players; blacks were banned by the National Baseball League, but blacks played in a separate Negro league that was not televised, or broadcast on radio. Columbus always said that the black players are just as good as the white players, some are even better, but they won't give them a chance to play in the major leagues. Someday, Columbus would say, a change will come; little black and white children will walk hand and hand to and from school, we will have black baseball players on television, and a black President of the United States; "I may not be around to see it, but my grandkids and their kids will see it."

Life for the black man is like the game of baseball, Columbus used to say, except you already have one or two strikes against you when you come up to bat; so you better hit a home run, because you only get one chance. Columbus felt that one strike was against you just because you are black, and most whites felt that blacks were inferior and less deserving, making them the privileged group. The second strike against you was because of your physical ability; many southern white men saw black men as intimidating. Some blacks were in better physical condition than some white baseball players because of all the heavy labour work blacks were forced to do as slaves. Black people were customarily the hardest and heaviest working class of people for many years; because they were forced to work the tobacco and cotton fields of America, farm the wheat and corn crops, take care of the livestock, and help build the bridges, roads, and railways. Black men fought in the Civil War for their freedom; and they were instrumental in making America what it is today.

Remember that in early slavery days, slaves were discouraged from learning to read or write, but required to speak English. To communicate, many blacks developed a sub-language using examples, patterns or models (paradigms) of child hood stories and sports to relay their messages. Stories like Burr Rabbit and Burr Fox, the Turtle and the Hare; always remember to keeping one goal in mind, the finish line; and don't be the last horse out the gate, don't strike out, step up to the plate and hit a homerun. My grandfather would say, make good marks in school and don't strike out at bat.

During my childhood and adult life, I could remember on more than one occasion being told by elderly black males that life for the black man can be compared to the game of baseball; you already have one strike against you, just because you are black. The elderly black men discussing the comparison of the black struggle and baseball were venting their frustrations and disappointment with the unequal treatment of Black men in America. One elderly black man was on his death bed at the V.A.

Hospital, in Seattle. I was his primary nurse. I could see the anger and sadness on his face, and hear it in his voice. White people do not want to see you do better, they want you to strike out every time; the bases are loaded against you from the start.

The paradigm of the black struggle and baseball, the analogy is that each strike at bat represents a civil rights liberty denied the black man throughout American History. Strike one represents equal opportunity to work and play in the national baseball league, on and off the field, equal opportunity to life, liberty and the pursuit of happiness. Equal opportunity to play was denied for many years just because of the colour of their skin; even though civil rights legislation had been passed to forbid discrimination. The Civil Rights Act of 1866 stated that all persons born in the United States were citizens, and had certain civil rights. The Fourteenth Amendment stated that all men are created equal, but there were still prevailing beliefs of white supremacy followers that economic, social and legal discrimination against non-white people was justified. White supremacy ideals were that all non-white people were inferior and equal opportunity could be denied.

Strike two represents equal protection under the law on and off the baseball field. The Fourteenth Amendment Section 5 stated that the congress has the power to enforce equal protection under the law for all citizens. Blacks players were citizens, yet players were not protected when they were assaulted for crossing the colour barriers on and off the baseball fields. Many blacks were living in fear, even in their own homes. The fear and stress of possibly being lynched were always present in their lives; lynching of blacks in the South went on unchecked until the civil rights movements of the 1960's.

Strike three represents equal representation on the baseball fields and in the American political decision making arena. Historically there were very few black players in baseball due to restrictions and colour barriers, and until recently blacks were systematically denied managerial and front office positions. Many baseball franchises in the past felt that blacks did not have the intellectual ability to be managers. This is called negative stereotyping. Negative stereotyping still exists today, in government and the political arena; many people feel that blacks are not intellectually capable to be good leaders.

The first African American to play in the Major Leagues was Jackie Robinson in 1947, but before Jackie, there were many great black baseball players who never received recognition for their performances. Players like Moses Fleetwood Walker, Bud Fowler, Satchel Paige and Josh Gibson. If you go online to www.negroleaguebaseball.com/history101, you can read that in 1867 the National Association of Baseball Players banned black players, just because they were black. There were a few black players in the minor leagues, but they had trouble playing in the south, because many places were off-limits for blacks. Hotels and restaurants had signs that stated 'no blacks allowed', fans would insult and throw things at them on and off the field.

Satchel Paige played for the New York Black Yankees in the 1930's. In September 1933, the New York Black Yankees played the Philadelphia Stars in the Coloured Championship of the Nation at Hinchliffe Stadium in Paterson, New Jersey. They lost the game, but, according to reports, they played great baseball, and played against some of the best players in the game, players like Josh Gibson, Jody Johnson and Cool Papa Bell.

The New York Yankees have won about forty World Series, more than any other team in history. In the 2009 World Series; they played, guess who, the Philadelphia Phillies, just like in 1933 and 1950.This rivalry continues today; the Yankees beat the Phillies four to two to win their 27th World Series. The Yankees usually pay more money to players, attracting some of the best talent. The Yankees have only won one Series in the last 15 years, and other teams are catching up.

In 2009 the New York Daily News wrote, "The 1950 Series will also be remembered for another reason, though not one either franchise is especially proud of. It was the last Fall Classic where every player from both teams was white. The Yankees and the Phillies did not embrace integration soon after Jackie Robinson broke the colour line with the Dodgers in 1947 and were among the last clubs to field a black player.

50 Years of Blacks in Baseball by Walter Leavy, an article written in 1995 in the Ebony magazine, stated that the Negro League was more exciting than the Major Leagues, because blacks utilized speed and stolen bases. Before blacks entered the Major Leagues, baseball was base to base, but blacks changed the concept, players like Jack Robinson in 1955, Maury Wills, Rickey Henderson and Lou Brock were fast and experts in stealing bases.When Hank Aaron broke Babe Ruth's home run record in 1974 with 715 home runs, he received hate mail and death threats from white fans who did not want a black to break the record. Blacks were denied front office and managerial positions until the 1990's, just like the black struggle, they were denied certain privileges.

In baseball today, the highest percentages of players are still white, then Hispanic, and then black. The percentage of black players in the major leagues keeps fluctuating, but we are starting to see a few black managers and pitchers. The reasons are partly because the majority of black athletic scholarships given by colleges are for basketball and football, more so than baseball. Colleges rarely draft straight out of high school, because they don't want to train a student. It all has to do with economics; there are more basketball hoops in the inner city than baseball fields, the college draft don't want to spend time and money on an athlete, they want them ready to play the game. Black kids in the inner cities have better opportunities to practice playing basketball and football, than baseball and golf.

In the game of baseball, like most sports, you have to be physically prepared, have strong arms and legs, quick reflexes and possess the speed and endurance to go the distance. We used to say as kids, when running track or playing ball; the ability to catch your second wind, lung capacity, is a skill you must learn if you want to be competitive. In the game of life, you have to be physically prepared to go the distance; black people inherited genes from their ancestors who were taught by experience that physical demands on the human body that don't kill you, can only make you stronger.

Chapter 2

Privileged and Non-Privileged Groups in America

During the Colonial and Revolutionary eras in American history, the early 18th Century, many southern white politicians and law-makers followed Herrenvolk Democracy, which was pro-south, pro-slavery, belief that the Declaration of Independence on July 4th 1776 was not referring to black people when it stated that all men are created equal. The good old boys club in congress created a white privilege by changing the interpretation of the Declaration of Independence; White people are equal to each other, but have superiority over non-whites. Many southerners felt that they were superior to black men; they wanted blacks to feel inferior and less deserving. Throughout history, white groups of males wanted to be privileged in all aspects of life, including sports and access to economic opportunities. White males were privileged; they enjoyed the right to vote, whereas blacks, Indians and women were not allowed. Privilege today means property and real estate, access to jobs, healthcare, housing, safe neighbourhoods and schools.

Black men were considered a threat to the privileged group of southern, white males, so the privileged group systematically would not give black men jobs, opportunities or allow them to own land or other properties. There were laws in some southern states during the Jim Crow Era that made it illegal for blacks to own property and land. Many properties were stolen from legal black land owners, insurance schemes involving city and state organizations to inhibit and confiscate all black owned land.

During the 18th and 19th Centuries, black women were allowed to work in service and labour jobs like kitchens and laundries; they were not seen as much of a threat to the privileged group, because they felt men are superior to women in general. White women were also considered second class citizens, so when the Women's Suffrage Movement began, advocating equality for women, and eventually giving women voting rights in 1920, this was instrumental in enforcing voting rights and civil right to blacks. The Fifteenth Amendment to the Constitution in 1870 gave black men the right to vote, yet they were denied access in most states, and women were considered unfit to vote. National attention was being given to women voting rights, which exposed the efforts of the south in preventing the black vote, such as not telling them about elections, rules like, to register you must own land and have a high school education.

Employment opportunities and income are major factors in providing and maintaining a stable family lifestyle. Even today, blacks are denied jobs; the unemployment rates are higher for black males than any other group in America. Historically, there has always been a large number of female head of households in the black communities. Financial matters and income has always been one of the main reasons many marriages do not work. Black men were not privileged; they were not allowed meaningful jobs to financially support and maintain a family. To enable the family to receive government assistance or other aid, some black men had no other options but to leave the family and go live with their own parents and relatives, or became homeless. Even today many marriages in the black community don't work because the black male cannot financially fulfil his role as the head of household. Many blacks made a career of the military, because they could not find a job anywhere else. Many blacks were murdered or sent to prison for long periods of time. The disruption of black families is a repercussion of past corrupt laws and correctional systems which penalized blacks more than any other race. The prison population, today and in the past, has always been predominantly black, not because blacks do more crime, but because blacks were routinely prosecuted for minor offenses. I have heard stories in the south of black men being sent to work farms and prison for five years for small petty crimes like stealing a watermelon or a chicken.

White newspapers in the past were negative to blacks; comments by the southern presses incited hostility against blacks, articles suggesting black males deserve to be beaten or lynched for looking at white women. All the time the privileged groups of white males were raping black women. Many White wealthy landowners had children by their black servants, and history speaks of George Washington and Thomas Jefferson having black children. Thomas Jefferson, according to rumours, had five children by his black slave, and when he died, he gave them their freedom. Just go to the internet and look up black children of George Washington and Thomas Jefferson.

Black people in the old days did not have any privileges, or equal protection of the Law. The Dred Scott Decision of the Supreme Court in 1857 defended the ruling that a black slave who once lived in a free state, or escaped to a slave free State from a slave state can be returned to plantation owners. If black slave owners sent bounty hunters after runaway slaves, all they needed were papers to show that the person was a slave at one time, they were considered personal property of someone who wanted them back; the law upheld this practice, stating that it was a violation of the Fifth Amendment to deprive the slave owners of personal property without due process.

During the 18th and 19th Centuries, immigrants that arrived in America, who faced discrimination in their own countries, found that in America they had privileges and rights not given to black people. This put them in a class above black people in America. The age of the common man, under Andrew Jackson's administration gave every American the right to vote and own property, excluding Blacks, Indians and women

In 2010 I had the privilege of taking care of an 87 year old Lithuanian cardiac intensive care patient at Providence Medical Centre. He told me that when he and a busload of contract labourers came to America in 1950, they had no housing arrangements and had to spend 18 hours on a bus outside a farm in Louisiana with no food or shelter. Black workers were the only people who came to their aid, brought them food and water; they had to sneak it to them, because if they got caught, they would be in trouble. He said he and all the other immigrants could not understand why southern whites treated black people so bad, that blacks were the kindest and nicest people in America. He said they signed a contract to work for 4 years, and then they were free to stay in America or return home to the old country. The workers were paid 11cents a day, and blacks made much less, some were not paid at all. They were told to stay away from the black people, and don't tell them what your salary was, because they would start asking for more. Unfair labour practices went on historically for black people, mostly in the private sectors; blacks would train non-blacks in a new job, then that person would later become their boss.

There are large populations of Lithuanian, Ukrainian, Poland and Russian immigrants in America today because their parents wanted to escape Nazi Germany and the Communist Soviet Union occupations of their countries during World War II in the 1940's. Lithuania was once the largest country in Europe, until it was taken over by other countries and divided up into smaller sections. They found out that by escaping to America, they could pursue the American dream, and had privileges not given to black, Indians and women in America; which put them in a class ahead of American minorities. Today many descendants of immigrants of lighter skin colours own property, private businesses and have better job opportunities than most blacks, Mexican, or other minorities of darker skin colour. Skin colour has always been a major factor in access to better economic opportunities in the history of our nation.

Chapter 3

Strong Religious Background

During the Slavery Era, the church was a sanctuary. Black gospel songs were written to tell a folk story. Some songs were secret messages to help slaves avoid capture, or ease the pain of oppression, torture and intimidations. Many songs provided comfort during long hours of working in the fields from sun up to sun down. As a child, our family was brought up in the church; my grandfather was a deacon, my grandmother active in the choir. Like many other southern black families, the church was an important part of our lives. Almost everyone in town went to church because they wanted to; it was their meeting place. The church provided a place of communication and expression, a community forum, a place to make announcements of upcoming events and share food and recipes. We all need a place of positive expression, a place to be safe, talk openly; when surrounded by negative experiences in life, especially if you have a long history of being suppressed, the church met that need.

The church provided many opportunities for the black community; the church taught community responsibility for raising children and keeping them safe. Schools were a top priority, improving the classrooms, finding qualified teachers, and providing new updated books. There were not many positive history books about black people in slavery days; most great achievements by blacks were accredited to whites for many years. In church we could talk about positive leadership in our black community and national accomplishments black people are making, and pray together for a better place in life. The church was the only recourse during hard times and diversities for many blacks in the past. Blacks depended on the church for spiritual wellbeing, and also a place to help others in need. When a disaster like a tornado strikes a small black community, there was usually no state or local assistance. Many people had to depend on community assistance, and the church was the primary resource. The church provided food and shelter in times of need, and was a sanctuary for runaway slaves or anyone in need. Hate groups targeted and burned black churches to discourage black progress, because the church was the foundation, the centrepiece.

Black gospel was a creation of its own; songs were not only about spiritual salvation and faith in god, but also of freedom from oppression, brutality and torture from the hands of white slave owners of the past. The suppressed blacks made up inspirational song like freedom to fly away from the shackles and chains, no more 50 lashes, and swing low sweet chariot. Songs about angels coming to take us home, to a place where we all are wealthy with love and find peace in heaven some day. We all remember from history classes that Harriet Tubman, a freedom fighter and civil rights leader, was one of the founders of the Underground Railroad. The Underground Railroad was an organization of free people, northern and southern, trying to help runaway slaves avoid capture and make it to freedom in the North. Many gospel songs like Freedom, Go down Moses, Heaven and Swing low were used as secret codes that only the slaves knew the hidden messages. Many great songs today reflect the history of the black struggle; and the roots for modern Blues, Jazz and Rock and Roll, were originally from church songs. Tom Dorsey, Sam Cook, Aretha Franklin, The Staple Singers and many more started out singing church songs.

Black people prayed for the day that America would have a black President; this would bring a feeling of pride and prosperity to black people, but not just for black people, all minorities; women, Indian, Asian and Latino as well. Most blacks have a history of religion in their background, because religion in the old days was a source of strength and peace of mind for oppressed people. In Luke 6:20-22 of the Holy Bible it says "Blessed are you poor for yours is the kingdom of heaven." The blacks in slavery times were the poorest people on earth; they were not compensated adequately for the work they performed. "Blessed are you that hunger, blessed are you that when men hate you and reveal you." Blacks were considered second class just because of the colour of their skin.

Most Americans consider themselves Christian, whatever religious denomination you consider yourself, Baptist, Lutherans, Methodists, Catholic or Jewish, we all believe in God. Traditionally I was raised in a Baptist church, but as an adult, I now worship with all denominations, because I feel that all religions should share a basic common interest of promoting love, unity and good will to all mankind. In the medical profession, religion is strongly encouraged. Religion is a strong and powerful support system, a phenomenon that has a positive effect on the outcome of patients' overall health and recovery from illness; through faith, miracles can happen, and have been known to happen.

Black people historically relied on the church for guidance and support, so when Martin Luther King, a Baptist minister, begin his campaign for racial equality, black people gave their support. King focused on the south, where they marched and protested non-violently. Martin

Luther King was the president of the Southern Christian Leadership Conference, which united southern ministers and churches to non-violently fight for civil rights in the early 1950's. King helped organize the Montgomery Bus Boycott in 1955 when Rosa parks refused to give up her seat and move to the back of the bus, which led to desegregating the public transportation systems throughout the south. Martin L. King was a great orator; during the 1963 March on Washington, in front of over 200,000 people he delivered his famous "I Have a Dream speech" which brought national attention to the need for civil rights reform, forcing President John F. Kennedy to write the new Civil Rights Bill of 1963.The new bill did not pass congress till 1964, because President JFK was assassinated after writing the bill. Dr. King, the great leader, had plans for other marches when he was assassinated in Memphis on April 3rd, 1968. He was planning a poor people's march to address economic conditions, lack of jobs and decent wages for all people; the march happened in June 1968, but was not a big a success as King had planned; because the great leader was gone.

Chapter 4

Living in Fear

Blacks during days of slavery and post slavery lived under conditions of constant fear and stress. Their overall health status as a race was damaged and compromised for generations to come by the waste food products they were forced to eat as slaves. They were forced to eat pig and cow guts, ears and feet; while their owners ate steak, and sent the rest to market. Blacks today have the highest rates of IDDM (diabetes) and HTN (high blood pressure) in the nation. Post slavery, blacks had to repair the nutritional damage to their bodies; so their basic food subsidies were mostly natural foods, home grown. Most blacks grew up eating vegetables out of their own gardens. They made bread from their ovens, and usually ate chicken, pigs and cows that they raised; because they did not want to go to town, where it could be dangerous. Why? Because they were living in fear of the possibility of being lynched.

Black people knew that they were second class citizens, and often faced harassment and intimidations from white people on the streets and at town markets; so they tried to stay away from public places. Blacks were constantly under considerable amounts stress related to money issues; because many could not read, write or count, and were often over-charged for commodities. Historically they were the lowest paid workers in our nation's history, many blacks had no job or only worked seasonally during plantation harvesting.

Many blacks were living in fear even in their own homes; the stress of being lynched was always present in their lives. According to Ida B. wells, "Our country's national crime is lynching. It is not the creature of an hour, the sudden outburst of uncontrolled fury, or the unspeakable brutality of an insane mob. It represents the cool, calculating deliberation of intelligent people who openly avow that there is an 'unwritten law' that justifies them in putting humans to death without complaint under oath, without trial by jury, without opportunity to make defence and without right of appeal. Lynch law in America 1900.Some states went as far as to give rewards to mob members for lynching black men, women and children who were considered "sassy niggers", if a black spoke out for equal pay, or got into a fight with a white, the black could get hung; if a white woman had consensual sex with a black man, the mob would hang the black man without a trial, claiming rape was involved, but if the woman was black and the man white, nothing was done. Blacks could not testify against whites in many states, which was unequal protection under the law; Arkansas, Louisiana, Tennessee and Alabama were leaders in black lynching's, many without criminal cause or a trial. You can see why most of the interracial children born in the south in the 18th and 19th Centuries were from white fathers and black mothers; of course rape was involved in most cases. The white community rejected the mixed race children, and forced them to live in black communities, because the old saying was that if you had 1/8th of black blood in your family, you are considered black, second class. With no state or local financial support for most black communities, they were economically disadvantaged in the early days, so they helped each other.

I can remember white people intimidating black kids in Fordyce for the fun of it; they wanted to see how afraid you got before laughing in your face. If you went to town to buy produce, you have to put up with white people being disrespectful to young black children, but they would not treat white children like that. If you hear a white person raising their voices at some black kids in a store, saying things like "hurry up and get what you want and get out, damn niggers don't do nothing but loiter." you can feel the tension of fear like a knife cutting through the air. Your sympathetic nervous system kicks in, giving you the flight or fight body response, your blood pressure goes up and your heart rate increases; the body's response to increased blood flow and oxygenation to your major muscle groups so they can go into action. When white people get angry with any blacks around public places, and start giving them the evil eye, many southern kids were taught to look down at your shoes and leave because an altercation could arise, and blacks were not often protected by the police.

The national mortality rates are higher for blacks suffering from heart attacks, hypertension diabetes and strokes; all related to lack of healthcare, diet and a long history of stress. You see more southern blacks suffering from stress related illnesses like heart problems and diabetes than northern blacks; this may have something to do with the longer periods of racial related stress issues, since southern blacks had to endure over a longer period of time than northern blacks. Lynching of blacks in the south went on unchecked until the civil rights movements of the 1960's; white and black civil rights workers were lynched in the south for supporting integration and voting rights. President John F. Kennedy signed into law the Civil Rights Act of 1964, which strongly supported equal protection under the law as guaranteed by the 14th Amendment in 1868.

Blacks in the South were always living in fear. If a person spoke up against injustice, black or white, they may get beaten, or assassinated; just look at what happen to Medgar Evers, John F Kennedy and Martin Luther King, they Stood up for Civil Rights and they were assassinated. The FBI closed the investigations early to protect the real culprits, the people who paid money to those dumb poor immigrants to assassinate an American icon. Many Blacks in 2008 did not want Obama to be elected because of fear that he may be assassinated. It is no wonder why so many blacks suffer from depression, unhappiness, and feelings of loss of hope, sadness, and being overwhelmed by the demands of the world.

Blacks have developed strong resilience, they can bounce back from adversities, and they use humour and music to ease the pain. There is an old saying of black people, my mother used to say it sometimes when things were not going as planned, "I have to keep laughing, to keep from crying." These defence mechanisms could explain why there are so many good black comedians, and blues singers.

I read a book once on Negro folklore by Langston Hughes, one of the short stories told about how many slave masters use to beat slaves to keep them in line, even pregnant women. They would dig a hole in the ground and have a pregnant female lay face down over the hole to fit the mom's stomach while she got her whipping. The slave masters wanted to protect the baby because there was good money in healthy black kids; they were needed to work the plantations and cotton fields. One story was humorous, about one feisty black woman, feisty even while pregnant, got a whipping one time while in late pregnancy, the hole they dug was big as a tin bath tub. She died giving birth in the cotton field. Ironic as it may sound, the person telling the story said it was his own mother. Everyone knows that it's no joke or laughing matter to beat a pregnant woman.

Throughout history it has been shown that dominant oppressive groups, in an effort to suppress and intimidate minority groups, would eliminate their leaders. The plantation owners of old days would forbid blacks from learning to read and write. They did not want blacks educated, for fear that they would fight for their rights to freedom. The most intelligent and strongest of males were removed, charged with a crime they did not commit, and sent off to work camps and prisons, or even murdered; systematically to eliminate the voices of strength, hope and encouragement for black children.

During the 18th Century, violence against blacks was not limited to the south, there were some states in the north were blacks were victims of racism and mob violence. Hate groups, criminal mobs and looters would rob black businesses, stores, churches and homes for their valuable possessions then burn the place down to cover up the evidence; there was no protection from law enforcement.

My mother would tell us stories about how in the old days, influential, strong black men would just come up missing one day, and no one has seen hide or hair of them since. Black males showing up missing, causes a downward snowball effect in the black community; the disruption of the black family structure Removal of the black male head of households creates a situation, putting more black families in poverty and leaving mothers as heads of households. The young males in most of these matriarch-led families will rebel against authority, because they don't have a black male role model to re enforce morality, right from wrong; all they know is basic human instinct, self-survival is the law of the land. I was taught in nursing school that psychosocially; children who grow up with insecure parental attachments develop pathologies like depression, compulsion and inhibitions of thought and expression. Family influences and support is very important to adolescents, without it they will seek out social support and acceptance from peer groups like street gangs. These kids are not bad kids, just a stage in human development they are going through; they need understanding, support and encouragement.

Do you remember learning in school about Maslow's Hierarchal of Human Needs? Take a look at Tabor's Medical Dictionary, or go online. To get to self-actualization, the ability to become all you are capable of becoming, you must first satisfy your basic human needs of hunger, safety, love, respect, and self-esteem. Many theories suggest that if you don't achieve the basic needs, you would have a difficult time achieving self-actualization. How can children achieve feelings of safety when family members, relatives and close friends were being shot down in the streets, or lynched? America would not stand by and watch children grow up in a war-torn region of the world, where death and violence is present on a regular day-to-day basis. Some children will have psychosocial problems for the rest of their lives, trust and fear issues. Psychosocial issues of fear and oppression causes stress; the diets slaves were forced to eat, which has an adverse effect on overall health for generations to come; is why black people, and all minorities, are deserving of free healthcare in America. America owes a debt, certain compensations, to Americans unintentionally put at healthcare risk, and they should be acknowledged. Universal Healthcare is the solution, not the problem or a blank check.

Chapter 5

Separate but Equal

In 1896 there was a significant case in the Supreme Court known as Plessy v. Ferguson the courts upheld racial segregation, saying that it is a constitutional right for states to segregate blacks from whites, even in public places like schools and railroads, as long the accommodations are equal. This landmark civil rights case created the separate but equal legal precedent for discrimination; and it continue in America for the next fifty years, until it is overturned by Brown v. Board of Education, 1954. Separate but equal was a tool used by the southern states to deprive black communities of federal aid and taxpayers' dollars.

I know from personal experience that black schools were inferior to white schools in the south. In the first grade I had a speech impediment, where I would pronounce the first word of a sentence twice. The teachers, therefore, held me back in the first grade, saying I could not read out loud in front of the class. Fortunately for me, my family moved to Denver, Colorado, where integrated schools had speech therapy. I started speech therapy, entered the second grade, and I was cleared of the speech impediment in months, and enjoyed reading out loud in front of the class.

I attended an integrated school in Denver Colorado in 1957, Crofton Elementary, but when my family moved back to the south five years later, I once again attended the all black school in Fordyce, Arkansas. Academically, everyone in my family was a year ahead of our classmates in Arkansas; when I was studying algebra in the eighth grade, they were studying long division. I made the Honour Roles weekly for having good grades; it was not a big deal to me.

Post slavery black America had to endure inferior communities, homes, schools and jobs for many years because the community had no voice, no decision making capabilities. Many Blacks did not own property; they rented the facilities, like homes, schools, and churches. Most of the rent went to improving the white community; they were separate, but not equal. Those separate but equal rules existed for many years, even after the famous landmark decision case of Brown v. Board of Education in 1954, which overturned Plessy v. Ferguson, stating that racial segregation was a violation of equal protection under the Fourteenth Amendment. In 1952 a suit was filed against the Board of Education, City of Topeka. Parents challenged the separate but equal rules, directed by the NAACP. As mentioned through this book, just because a law was passed, did not mean that the southern states would abide by the laws, many schools in small southern towns are still separate and unequal today.

The wealth of the nation is deeply rooted in real estate property and land ownership. Blacks during the early post slavery days in America was disadvantaged in accumulating wealth. Jim Crow laws in most southern states forbade black people to own land and property. Land is an asset which rarely depreciates, if blacks had ownership of half the land that was stolen from their ancestors there would be less poverty in the black community, and wealthier black Americans.

My mother said that her father told her when military soldiers would come home from the war, some of the white folk would attack them and throw things at them or spit on them, and say things like, "look at those uppity niggers, think they are good as us, have a right to be in uniform."

Most of the professional jobs in my mother's home town of Fordyce, Arkansas when she was growing up were for white people only; the lawyers, doctors, bank owners and real-estate agents were all white; we never saw a black doctor or insurance agent. There were no black plumbers or carpenters because it was so difficult to get licensed, you had to belong to the plumbers' union or carpenters' union to get a license; but no blacks are allowed to be union members per rules of the union. There was nothing for the black man to do but work in the fields or the saw mill. Many Blacks found handyman jobs for food or cash; but this income is not considered for social security, unemployment and retirement compensation. Land was stolen from black in many ways in the old days, if you are late on your taxes, white people would get together and pay the taxes, call it a homestead act and put the land up for auction, there were no equal housing lenders to help black people in trouble with back taxes.

Many southern states after the civil war sometimes ignored federal laws, did not agree with our nation's leaders, or the knowledge and wisdom the Lincoln administration had to offer. Abraham Lincoln's famous Gettysburg address quoted that all men are created equal, but many southern states continued to discriminate; they withheld resources designated to improve the black communities, left the black community, facilities, and schools in second class condition.

In Fordyce, the black community had two small stores, McKenzie's and Pam's; and the white community had two bigger stores, Crowder's and Mad Butcher. I remember as a child my grandmother Ella Lee Thrower, who loved watching Gunsmoke, starring James Arness as Mat Dillon, and Chester; and The Days of Our Lives, eating vanilla ice cream and chewing juicy-fruit gum. Grandma would give me a list of things to buy at the store, and say "go to the white store, because the black stores sometimes don't carry very much; and be nice, say yes sir and no sir". The stores, and everything else were separate, but they were not equal.

Chapter 6

Systematic Discrimination

Systematic discrimination for minorities existed in the job markets, military, housing, healthcare and many other government agencies pre and post slavery era; and some traces of its remnants still exist today. Rules and regulations were designed to disadvantage certain groups, even the legal system in some states made it illegal for a black to testify against a white person in a court of law. Black men, especially, were taught not to trust white politicians or doctors, because of past unfair treatment in employment and healthcare. Have you heard of the Tuskegee Syphilis Study? This was where the U.S. Public Health Services, conducted a study using 399 poor African-American sharecroppers from Alabama who had syphilis to conduct a research study from 1932 to 1972. In 1947 penicillin was found to be effective in treating syphilis, but the scientist decided to withhold it from the blacks, to watch the progression of the disease. Many of the men died horrible deaths, and their wives and children contracted the disease. This was an ethical issue that led to federal regulations for the protection of human subjects during research.

When black men and women get second class treatment in hospitals, this is systematic discrimination, and it exists. I have personally witnessed white patients getting pampered and groomed in hospitals while the few black patients get neglected; it is all about racism and finances, what services your insurance coverage will or will not pay for. A government controlled healthcare systems is desperately needed to prevent unequal medical treatment in the healthcare industry.

In many hospitals today, medical treatment is not based on healthcare needs, but healthcare insurance, what you can afford to pay, and once you reach your limit, you may get kicked out on the street. The healthcare insurance cost has skyrocketed in the past few years, leaving millions of Americans without healthcare coverage. Profit motivated healthcare agencies, pharmaceutical companies and malpractice suits keep raising the prices, creating a form of systematic discrimination against the poor and unemployed.

I read an article in The Stranger September 11, 2008, a weekly Seattle publication article, a perfect example of racial profiling. The author talked about how the Seattle City Council in 2007 requested a racial disparities report on youth arrested in Seattle for marijuana possession; the report showed that black youths were arrested 75% more than their white counterparts. The article stated that, "more black people than white people continue to be arrested and prosecuted for marijuana possession in Seattle, according to data from the City Attorney's Office. The recent data reflect a pattern of racial disparity announced in January, when a city council-appointed panel released a report on marijuana enforcement between 2000 and 2006". Marijuana should have been legal years ago, profit motivated special interest groups working for the tobacco and alcohol industries are fighting legalization. Let's save some tax payers dollars, stop building more jails, put an end to the racial profiling of young black youths, and redirect our crime prevention efforts to producers and suppliers of illegal dangerous addictive drugs like cocaine and heroin. Many blacks were prosecuted under the Three Strikes Laws designed to keep violent offenders off the streets, because blacks did not have adequate legal representation. In many cases the court appointed public defenders did not want to spend a lot of time on a case, they wanted to close as many court cases as possible, as fast as they can, and move on to the next. With a felony conviction, you lose many rights of citizenship; the right to vote and drive a car; and most of the young black males coming out of prison, have a difficult time finding a job and supporting a family.

Everybody knows that large amounts of illegal drugs on the streets in America are imported from other countries like Europe, Thailand, Mexico, Jamaica and South America. It takes huge financial support systems to transport these drugs across the borders by airplanes, boats and underground networks. Most black youth don't have these kinds of networks, yet they are prosecuted more than any other group. The black kids did not have summer jobs, they needed money to survive, but the Reagan administration cancelled a lot of those programs, black parents did not own their businesses, or have relatives and friends who own their own businesses to put black youth to work for the summer like many white families could. Why are we prosecuting people for using natural products that has never legally been determined hazardous to human health like tobacco and alcohol which is addictive and killing people, so addictive that they need treatment to stop? Most people grow out of marijuana use as they get older; it's a thing many people tried when they were younger in college; unless using it for a medical condition like pain, depression, glaucoma, eating disorders and cancer. According to a recent internet article, cannabis hemp products have been around since 8,000BC,

Christopher Columbus carrier hemp seeds on his fleet, US presidents Thomas Jefferson and George Washington were both hemp farmers for the textile industry, and Benjamin Franklin used cannabis hemp in his paper mill. I was watching a cop show on TV a while back, when there was gang activity, or gang fights; if the participants are black or minority, they are all going to jail. When two white rival groups of youth met up to fight in a predominantly all white upscale community, the police had a different attitude about enforcing the law. Double standards existed, as if the police were counselled on protecting the white fighters from going to jail, no one was arrested, and they all were given warnings. The point is that historically it is customary in police departments to arrest blacks and other minorities for crimes that most whites would not get arrested for. July 2009, a prominent black Harvard professor, Henry L. Gates Jr. was arrested inside his home for being loud and unruly. He had just returned from a working trip to China, could not get his front door open, and a neighbour thought he was a burglar, and called the police. It was an obvious lack of communication, which possibly would not have happened if he was white. I had a similar situation, when working the night shift, I got home from the V.A. Hospital at 1am, it was trash pickup day, so I took my trash from the back to the front, and a neighbour called the police and said there was a prowler at my house. The police surrounded my house with guns drawn and put me in handcuffs before finding out the story. They would not let me go into my house for identification, and would not release me until they knocked on the door and my wife came out to identify me. I had to yell at my dog (a tan German Sheppard Mix) to lie down; for fear that they will shoot him if he would not let them in to search around the house. Don't get me wrong, I am not prejudice against white people, and I think it is admirable that neighbours look out for each other and keep the community safe. Do you see the disparity? Come on now, you have watched cop shows on television, do police always put handcuffs on suspects before finding out the situation, or just black men in predominately white neighbourhoods?

Black people know from experience that when they file a medical or auto insurance claim, if your name sounds black or if you mark your race as black, you can be sure the claim is rejected the first time, or sent for review, because most agencies in the past were trained to be suspicious of black or other minority claims. On the other hand, a white person filling the same claim for the same reasons will be accepted, no questions asked. As a black person you can buy an item of clothing from a department store then decide you want to exchange it because it doesn't fit, the clerk will tell you it's been worn, or you don't have the receipt, or we just don't take returns, whereas if you were white, and bring it back one week later without the receipt, they will take it back no questions asked.

I can remember even in the late 1970's, there were clear documentation of discrimination in housing; it was all over the news, some agencies would send out a black couple to buy a house in an upscale neighbourhood, they have all the qualifications and cash, but the property owners would inflate the price or tell them the property was sold yesterday. The next day the agency would send a white couple to buy the same property, and the property owners would sell the property on the spot without the necessary closing expenses.

There is a strong connection between adequate housing and health. The world population continues to rise, and more people move into cities. This creates inner city congestion and housing shortages. Inner city housing shortages create inadequate living conditions like substandard plumbing and electrical systems. When there is a lack of black plumbers and electricians, this puts the black community at risk for increased health problems. The overall health of the black community is negatively affected by inadequate housing, and overcrowding, which is associated with unsafe drinking water, and poor air quality. I read an article once where a black housing project was built over a toxic waste dump, the residents were sick all the time. It is a known fact that access to decent housing, safe neighbourhoods, good schools, useful contacts and other benefits is largely influenced by the community in which one is born, raised and resides.).The article went on to say more blacks live in the city than whites, about seventy percent of white families own their own homes, compared to fifty percent for black. With these multitude of health risks existing in the black communities, there is no wonder people are sicker in the cities; there are more allergies, more airborne infections, pollution from factories and automobiles. Viruses like the flu and pneumonia are easily spread between people in close contact with others. The low income people and the homeless, who already are disadvantaged by not having adequate healthcare, can't escape the city by moving to the suburbs, because they cannot afford the mortgages.

Modern day systematic discrimination exists in community house pricing, exclusive neighbourhoods cater to the rich and famous; if you don't have a million dollars, you can't live in this neighbourhood. There is hope on the horizon; we may start to see a change in the way people think about race relations, housing discrimination and healthcare coverage in the United States. When you have people of colour, women and other minorities in high positions of authority, like President of the United States, Supreme Court Justices, or Secretary of Health and Human Services, it would be very difficult for systematic discrimination to continue unchecked in America.

Chapter 7

Growing Up in the South

My grandfather was from the old school, he lived in southern times when black people had to be self-supportive. He had lots of chickens; we ate eggs every morning and had chicken every Sunday after church; he also had a couple of horses, a mule, and planted his own cornfield and vegetable garden. Grandpa and a few of his closest friends would go hunting on occasions, and they would bring home large deer, cut them up, divide up the meat and store it in a smoke house for the winter. He provided for himself and family, and did not go to the grocery store much, just for basic items like flour salt and sugar.

When we were little children, about 4 years old, my brother Larry and I used to play cops and robbers on tricycles with a little white boy from the white community. As we got older, that activity was discouraged by the white and black communities. Soon he stopped coming around; Larry and I did not see him as a white boy, someone we were not supposed to play with; we just saw him as our cops and robbers playmate. I thought I was Mighty Mouse in the first and second grade; I watched too many cartoon heroes on television. If a girl was being bothered, I would come to the rescue.

When I was 12 years old I talked my mother into letting me stay with grandpa and grandma in Fordyce; I said that I could be a big help around the house; running errands to stores and to other relatives for them. I went down for the summer and ended up staying for more than a year. I was treated as a like an only child; I had the best clothes, own room, and money; grandpa use to say, "Son, a man should always have money in his pocket." I was with grandpa when he died at home in his own bed in 1962; he hardly ever went to see a doctor. Most black people in the old days did not have medical or dental healthcare coverage, and many did not trust doctors and hospitals.

My grandpa told me on his death bed, "don't cry son, when the lord calls, and it your time to go, it's okay. It's all in God's hands now. You will have to be the man around the house when I'm gone." When the rest of the Thrower-Williams family and relatives come to town for the funeral; I tried very hard to be strong, I fought back the tears; but I could not for long, I cried. I realize now that sometimes, it's better to release your emotions, and let your body emotionally heal through the natural grieving process.

Some of my greatest memories as a child in the south were waking up at 4 AM in the morning, packing a sack lunch and going hunting or fishing with my grandfather. He only took me on short hunting or fishing trips. We walked for half hour, and was usually back by noon, and grandma would have dinner cooking. Grandpa treated me like a man, explaining why catfish stick closer to the banks and trout and bass are out in the middle of the lake. Most of all I really enjoyed the scenery, skies were always sunny and blue, birds chirping along the way, through the forest and down the beautiful river banks. We usually looked for cat fish, rabbit or other small game. We always came home with something; kind of made you feel like you are taking care of the family.

Grandpa had a couple of guns, a .22 long rifle for hunting, and a shotgun; he also had lots of fishing gear, and loved to fish. He gave me my first pocket knife and first cup of Coffee at 12 years old. He said, "Son, you have to be alert to every sound and movement when you go out hunting the woods." Grandpa and Mom use to tell us all the time to hold your head up high, be proud of where you came from. If you see wrong being done, speak out against it; it's better to die fighting on your feet like a man, than crawling on your knees; the bigger they are, the harder they fall. I had an uncle named T.C. Thrower, who loved to travel; he always told us that "It isn't about where you are from that matters in life, it's about where you are going that really counts."

Country boys and girls learned how to make most of their own toys. Girls made dolls, clothes and jump ropes. The girls always played with jacks and a ball, while boys played with marbles. Girls often played house with small dishes, cookies and cool aid while boys played cowboys and Indians or cops and robbers. Boys often made toy guns, slingshots, bow and arrows and match guns; you could injure someone with some of those toys if you are not careful. The match gun, a toy we used to make by turning a clothespin around backwards with the spring pulled back; tie with a rubber band, put a wood match in, then push the spring. It would fire, sending a lit match at least five to ten feet. I wouldn't advise this because it is very dangerous playing with fire.

One day we almost set fire to an entire field; testing to see how far the match will go. The fire department had to be called; the fire started getting out of control, so we ran like hell. Country kids found whatever they could find to play on, trees, logs, and train tracks. We use to like playing on parked trains; we once released the brakes on a single boxcar on a hill. It started to roll down the hill, and finally crashed into a loading dock; boom, 'making a loud collision-like sound! We ran, and never looked back; and never told our parents what we had done.

Grandpa was a marksman; he could knock the head off a snake at 100 feet, and shoot a rabbit on the run. On one occasion I could remember myself and several other small children playing in the front yard, and a huge black snake kept creeping closer and closer to the smallest kids; the snake would hide behind a tree, then move closer to a bush, then move closer to a flower stand not far from the smallest kids. We did not see the snake, but my grandfather did; he went into the house and came back with his gun. We heard a loud boom, my ears were ringing, with one shot the snake was dead, and his head was torn completely off. My mother held the snake up with a stick; no joke, it must have been at least five feet long.My mother use to tell stories of snakes that can whistle like a human, and some snakes that can even move faster than a small child. Mom said when you are walking in the woods late at night; always sing a song or whistle, letting other animals know you are coming; when you surprise wild animals at night, that's when they will attack you.

One time I was playing in the woods with a sling shot, 12 years old, shooting at rabbits, squirrels and birds. I had my pocket knife and my faithful dog Sheik with me, so I wasn't afraid of anything. Sheik was a great dog, big, part lassie and old yeller type dog; he always comes when you call him. Everybody wanted that dog when I moved back to Denver, he was fast, obeyed commands, and could jump fences. As we went deeper into the woods that day, Sheik started acting nervous, I felt that we were being watched, or even stalked. As I whistled and walked along, I had visions of being Davie Crocket; killing a bear at only three, with just a pocket knife going through my head. Suddenly sheik started growling and took off running toward the sounds; I called him back, then he came shooting out of the bushes, running the other way. Of course, I followed him. We made to the edge of the woods, and looked back. Sheik was still slightly growling; we both felt that something was there, but we did not stick around to find out what.

My mother told us that one time a life insurance collector came to our house, and was raising his voice at my grandmother for being late on a life insurance payment; he did not know that my grandfather was home. Grandpa came to the front door and told the collector not to shout at his wife, the collector said if she would pay her bills on time, he would not have to come out here.My grandfather reached above his head, above the doorway, where he kept his double barrelled shotgun, and brought it down. Mom said that the insurance collector fell down twice while running before he made it to his old Model-T Ford. That insurance collector never came back; he went to the sheriff; told him that grandpa pointed a shotgun at him. The sheriff knew my grandfather, and told the agent to be careful how you talk to some people.

Mom said that a long time ago, our uncle Toot got in trouble with the law; they chased him to my grandfather's house, where he hid in the attic. The police told my grandfather, if you see Toot, bring him down to the station tomorrow. Uncle Toot caught a midnight train to St Louise; he came back 10 years later and built a small home on the Steele family property, next to our property. Mom also said that our father, Walter Williams, got in trouble with the law; had to leave town once because he cut a man from ear to ear in a fight. The police again came to my grandfather's house and asked him if he had you seen Walter, and grandpa said "no, but when and if I see him, I will have him come down." Dad, also like uncle Toot, had to leave in the middle of the night. Sometimes when hostilities and problems arise in small towns, you have to leave until things cool down.

Grandpa instilled the importance of owning and keeping property in the family; our family still owns those sections of land in Fordyce, Arkansas today. Mother, the story teller; said that everyone in the town knew that Papa did not play games with people, no one would ever think about coming on this property raising their voices with the intent of harming anyone; Papa would not allow that. Mom said that if Papa told you to hit the road, you better hit the road, get to getting, quick, fast and in a hurry. You have to remember that in those days, the law did not protect black people from lynch mobs you were on your own. Most lynchings occurred away from home; they caught people at work or on your way home. Black people would fight to the death in their own homes to stay alive. Mom used to say "they may take you out, but you better take a few of them out with you; I'll bet the next time they won't be so quick to jump".

Black and white kids did not go to school or play together in most small southern towns in 1950; it was the culture of the South. As far back as I can remember as a child, the schools in the south were substandard, most of the books were used; but the school faculty did a good job educating children with what they had. My father was your average saw mill factory worker and military veteran; when the saw mill occasionally closed or laid off workers, families suffer. Jobs were scarce for black men in those days; women sometimes could find work when men could not. My mother was smart, beautiful, and charismatic; she took nursing classes in Littlerock at an early age, before she was married. She wanted to leave the south so her kids could get an education and have better opportunities in life. Schools were segregated, all of our teachers were black, all of our classmates were black, and the only associations with white people were in the grocery stores or in town, walking on the street.

I miss my grandfather and father sometimes; Dad was not the woodsman like grandpa, but he loved us and tried to do his best taking care of us. I could remember, as a small child, Dad coming home dusty and smelling like saw dust before taking a bath; me and my younger brother Larry, used to use his arms as pillows before falling to sleep. Dad used to take us to fun places like carnivals and boating on the lake; but mom did not like us being on the water with Dad if he'd had a drink, she said it was dangerous. When my father and mother separated in 1956, my father and the three older kids remained in Arkansas, while my mother and the four younger kids moved to Denver, Colorado. A year later Mom sent for the other three older kids. We often return to the south, Arkansas, where my grandparents lived and North Carolina where my father lived; we were able to observe some of the attitudes and difficulties of growing up southern compared to northern, first hand.

The southern black kids were fearful of discriminatory laws and policies in the south, curfew laws were often directed towards blacks, while very few white kids got arrested for violating a curfew. If there were any altercations between black and white youth, the authorities would rule in favour of the white kids, because it was their custom in the south, the way things have always been done. In the South, most white people would openly admit to your face that they are prejudice, and don't like your kind, and you could see it in their actions.

When shopping at a department store or grocery store, most white clerks would throw items at you, and if you have change coming, they won't hand it to you, but throw it on the table. There were no mixed black and white clubs, interracial dating was illegal, and if you got in trouble with the law, you can bet you won't get a fair trial, because there were no black lawyers. If you stole a chicken in the Deep South to feed your family, the law for stealing livestock can be applied, so instead of a misdemeanour of petty theft, a person can be charged with a felony, and sentenced to five years' hard labour on a work farm.

Several years later, while living in Colorado, in 1961, my grandfather died, and the whole family returned Arkansas for the funeral. It was then that the members of my family decided to remain in the south for a while, because the cost of living was cheaper, and a little money could go a long way. A lot of things had not changed, the conditions of the schools were still substandard and segregated; it seemed like the government was keeping the black community in a time warp, held in suspended animation, all dirt roads and train tracks. There was nothing for kids to do, no social programs, no community centres, state and local funding for those programs went exclusively to the white community. If you weren't on the track or basketball team, you had very little to do except play cards or horseshoes. The school had no funding to buy equipment for baseball or football.

During the Martin Luther King Jr. era, 1955-1968, change still had not come to the black south; lots of injustices still existed, like coloured and white only eating establishments, blacks still rode in the back of the bus. It was the southern way of life, and blacks were being financially discriminated against, often overcharged for second class goods and services.

There were no black doctors in the majority of southern towns in 1950; so most blacks did not go to the doctor unless it was a matter of life or death. Black males got the worst medical treatment, because they were considered second class citizens and many white doctors and nurses were prejudiced. Many black men do not go to hospitals today because in the past they were often misdiagnosed or intentionally became the victims of malpractice and experimental surgeries. We discussed the Tuskegee Syphilis Studies, where black men were part of a research project, supposedly being treated for syphilis over a 20 year period, but was never given the drug Penicillin, which could have eradicated the disease, but scientists withheld this medication from them because they wanted to see what the disease would do to the human body untreated; most of the airmen became blind before dying. There were a few jobs in the small southern towns for blacks in the 1960-1980's; the stronger males worked at wood mills or train yards, women worked as maids, some worked in fields or factories at less than minimum wage. The cost of living was cheap, a few dollars could go a long way, rent was cheap, and you could live in a decent place for the money you make on a less than minimum wage job.

Martin Luther King Jr. was a true leader in the African American civil rights movement. A respected Baptist Minister from Atlanta, Georgia and President of the Southern Christian Leadership Conference, Martin led the 1955 Montgomery Bus Boycott, and the 1963 March on Washington, where he delivered his famous "I Have a Dream" speech. Dr King brought awareness to the world that although civil rights laws have passed, the south continued to discriminate, and the federal government did nothing. Where was the equal protection under the law? Discriminatory violations in the south needed to be enforced. Dr King was assassinated on the 4th April 1968 in Memphis, Tennessee. In the 1960's the NAACP with Medgar Evers, and President John F Kennedy, played an instrumental role in passing the Equal Employment Opportunity Act, and Civil Rights Act of 1964, which forbid discrimination based on sex, race or religion in hiring, promotion or firing practices. There was a lot of tension between blacks and whites; Medgar Evers was assassinated at his home in 1963, and then a few months later President John F Kennedy was assassinated in Texas.

The southern blacks were dealing with a different set of problems than northern blacks; the Civil Rights Movement was alive and strong, threats of violence and hostility exist in their everyday lives, but in the north, civil rights violations were not as bad; the youth had equal opportunity and were working together with whites to protest and end the war in Vietnam. Relatives in the south told me that the state and local government did little for the veterans returning from war, there were no outreach programs to ensure that the veterans received their entitlements like home and educational loans, but the white kids got homes and went to college. It was not until about 1972 that the small town of Fordyce, Arkansas started to integrate its schools, blacks started going to the white school and whites started going to the black school. Change in the way people think about other races did not improve until they started going to school together, where they could see with their own eyes that there is good and bad in any race.

In the 1970's, I visited a small college town in Lawrence, Kansas with a former girlfriend of mine, Patty Lindsay, a black girl, mother of two small, beautiful kids, Tiffany and Cassidy. We drove down to visit her mother and father for one week during the summer. That small town reminded me of Fordyce, like stepping back in time, going through a time warp, and it was just an hour away from a big city. There were little shacks on cylinder blocks and dirt roads; her dad took me deep into the woods to meet the moonshiners, where we got a free clear fruit jar of moonshine.

Chapter 8

Growing Up in the North

Moving out of the south was quite an experience, I noticed a change in the atmosphere on race relations, attitudes of blacks and whites; the people were friendlier, and you got the feeling when talking to most white people, that they genuinely liked you as a person, and respected what you had to say. The schools were great, with new classrooms, new books, new equipment, indoor basketball courts and pools. The schools were fully integrated, there were black and white teachers, class mates were a mixture of all nationalities, and you got the opportunity to see other people as not just races, but unique individuals of a different race.

When my other brothers and sister united with us in Denver a year later, I could notice a difference; they had a lot of mistrust for white people, they had no white friends, while we all thought most white people were okay. It was obviously a cultural difference that took them a while to grow out of. The black kids in the north were less fearful of discriminatory laws directed at blacks because there was less discrimination, and most blacks didn't tolerate disrespect from white people. If a black kid had an altercation with a white kid for calling him a derogatory name or something like that, the authorities would handle it fairly, whereas in the south, the black kid would always be in trouble.

We grew up in the church as children; but that is not saying that we were perfect angels. In most large families like ours, there was always something going on. We got our fair share of spankings when we were little, but there also were a few things we got away with. The streets were tough, but we were some of the toughest kids on the block. We were kind of like the Ma Barker and sons of the Old West; with five boys, and two girls, mom use to say "if one of you gets beat up, you all get beat up, stick up for each other, and don't go down without a fight." Mom always said that two is always stronger than one. No one in the projects would mess around with the Williams'; there was just too many of us, they would have to fight us all. I was a negotiator in block disturbances and would always stick up for the underdog; if a person is outnumbered or being bullied, black, white or brown, I would step in; I was raised that way. I got beat up a few times sticking up for people, but like mom used to say, if it don't kill you, it can only make you stronger.

My mother, Frances, was a hard-working, strong, single black parent who raised seven kids in the projects of Denver, Colorado. Mom, as a nurse and later as a social services worker, helped many people: disadvantaged single mothers, friends and relatives. She was a very good judge of character and had friends of all nationalities. She treated everyone with love and respect; and many people came to her for advice.

Frances was a great story teller, just like her mother. She could take a room full of children, captivate their attention and tell them stories with significant underlining educational meanings to life. She made her stories so interesting, all eyes would be on her, there would be total silence, so you could hear a pin drop when she spoke.

Mom told stories about Burr Rabbit, the Fox, the Turtle and other talking animals. Burr Rabbit represented black people, and the Fox represented white people. Mom said you have to use your brains and stay one step ahead of white people who mean you no good. She made it very clear that not all white people are bad, but some are. The Fox caught Burr Rabbit, and Burr Rabbit said, "You can eat me, but please don't throw me in the briar patch." Just before the Fox ate Burr Rabbit, he was convinced that it would be better to torture him first by throwing him in the briar patch, then eating him. Burr Rabbit was actually born in the briar patch; he knew that the Fox could never catch him there. Another story about the Turtle and the Rabbit, where the Turtle represented black people and the Rabbit was white people who mean you no good. The Turtle kept his eyes on the prize, the finish line, freedom; while the Rabbit kept getting distracted by the many pleasures along the way, thinking he had plenty of time to do what he come here to do so he lost the race.

Mom believed that education was the key to success, her main reason for wanting to leave the South was a better education for her children. Mom encouraged all her children to complete high school and go on to college. Mom use to say that the government and legal system can take every materialistic thing you own, but some things they can never take away from you is your faith in God, love for others, education and support from family.

I attended the University of Colorado, and graduated from Metropolitan State College in Denver and the University of Washington, WA. My sister, Paulette, attended Colorado State University, and graduated from Metropolitan State College, CO. My brother Walter attended Community College Red Rocks and Denver University. My other brothers and one sister, all furthered their educations through community colleges and other trade schools.

The great beloved Williams family matriarch, Frances L. Williams, passed away at home in Denver, Colorado, November 8th 2010, three days before her 89th birthday. Surrounded by family and loved ones, she will be deeply missed, but not forgotten. There was a large family birthday party at my sister Paulette's house on Veterans Day, November 11th, her birthday, in her honour. At her funeral the ministers and choir were her own family. Minister Ronnie Williams, her son, led us in prayer, Minister James Allen Davis, her grandson, gave a eulogy that brought us all to tears, and the Williams family choir did a spectacular job, they sang their hearts out, brought the church to their feet; Elder Louis Gene Washington, who was like one of her own children, read from the Old and New Testament. He knew her personally, like most kids in the neighbourhood; when he was a troubled youth, before he found God, he ran to my mother's house one night and told her that he had been shot in the chest, she told him to stop running and lay down, she applied pressure and called 911, but he would not be calm; probably wanted to see his family, ran out before the ambulance arrived. He lived to tell the story, because he lived a half block away, and found God, who helped change his life around.

In the 1950's, there were a lot more social programs and community activities provided to northern kids than to southern kids, there were local community centres, summer youth camps, Boy Scouts, Girl Scouts, and Job Core. There were mixed white and black schools, dance clubs, and more job opportunities for blacks. Economically, you could make more money in the north because minimum wage was higher, so if a person had a decent job, he could make much more money doing the same job in the north than in the south.

In the 1960's The YMCA and Red Cross were active in the black communities, providing services like summer youth programs; there was Job Corp and Youth leadership;

73

a lot of activities to keep you busy and out of trouble. The Vietnam War brought people together; there was a sense of unity to a common goal of working for peace and democracy worldwide.

Throughout grade school and college, our teachers were racially diverse; we had teachers of all nationalities. All of the teachers in the Denver school board of education system were dedicated, competent educators. The teachers all seem to have a deep professional commitment for the success of the students, regardless of race or nationality. At Manual High School, in 1968, the instructors who taught sports, basketball, football, baseball, tennis and golf were professionals in their fields, they actually played the sport; so we were impressed as children, because they really knew what they were talking about.

The Principal at Manual High School, James D. Ward was a great leader, dedicated to equal education and opportunities for blacks and other minorities. We were taught the most valuable gifts of humanity; that is to love and respect all people, and not stereotype people because of differences in race or culture.

Our community leaders, like William (Bill) Roberts, supported all the youths in the community as if they were his own kids. Bill Roberts, as director of the neighbourhood community centre, helped provide activities like basketball, football and boxing. He also provided personal assistance and guidance for neighbourhood kids, to keep them focused on school and out of trouble with the authorities. If a kid from the neighbourhood needed something, you could count on Bill Roberts to help; he co-signed for me on my first car at sixteen, to help me get back and forth from a summer job folding boxes.

My entire family always spoke out against wrong doing and racial injustices, that's just how we were raised. I often stood up for other kids who were bullied at school, or just needed a friend in the community. I got expelled from high school a few times for being involved in fighting. Kids can be very hard on new kids coming into a new school for the first time; I was the new kid several times. Usually I would try to be a peace keeper, a negotiator during disputes, but if push comes to shove and my brothers were around, Luther and Walter, there would be a fight.

My brothers believe in fighting first and asking questions later. As kids growing up, my brothers and I would use boxing gloves to settle disputes. We got boxing gloves one Christmas, and we would play with toy guns for a while then play with our boxing gloves. As a boxer, you need to know how to cover up, protect your face; and when you throw a punch, you have to step into the punch, bringing more power to the point of contact. Footwork and body positioning is also very important; some fighters can tell when you about to throw a punch just by the position of your feet.

There were a few good boxers that came out of Globe Ville; our old neighbourhood as teenagers growing up. Golden Glove armature boxing was popular in Denver; usually there was a weekly boxing ring set up at the community centre, and young inspiring boxers could work on improving their skills. There was my brother Walter Williams, Gene Washington, James Grimes and Ron Lyle. Now all these guys were fast and could hit hard, too. My brothers used to say, "The person that gets the first solid punch in usually wins the fight."

My brother Walter later became an international boxer on his U.S. Army boxing team. The family went to see one of his fights in Denver; he had to fly all the way from Germany while on active duty for that fight. It was like the Mohamed Ali and Ken Norton fight; a tough fight. Walter lost by a split decision; the fans got what they paid for, a good fight. The entire fight was pretty even; both fighters showed good boxing skills. There were no knockouts; although Walter knocked his opponent down once.

One of my best friends was Raymond Lyle, had a brother, Ron Lyle, who got mixed up with the gangs at an early age, and ended up going to prison for attempted murder. Ron had street fighting skills, a brawler, so when he went to prison, he perfected his boxing skills by working out in the ring a lot. Ron fought Mohamed Ali on May 16th 1975; and was winning on all the judges' cards until the 11th round. That's when Mohamed Ali got serious and stopped playing around with the rope-a-dope. Ali Met Lyle in the centre of the ring and traded punches; then one strong right hand from the champ, and it was all over except for the cheering. Lyle did not know what hit him, like a ton of bricks, it came out of nowhere. Lyle was in trouble, but he still did not go down; then a flurry of lightning fast lefts. The referee had to stop the fight, Lyle was defenceless; and Ali was setting him up for another right hand. Ron Lyle continued to fight for many years after that historic fight. Many other good fighters have often stated that Ron Lyle was one of the toughest fighters they had ever faced; including George Foreman in 1976.

One time at Cole Junior High school in Denver, Colorado, two bullies were harassing kids on the play field, they were 8th graders, and we were 7th graders, it did not matter to me that they were bigger and older; I still told them to knock it off. They wanted to fight me after school, so we met at the park after school. The kids formed a circle for us to fight in; the only option was to fight; lucky for me, my brothers showed up. My brothers told me to just walk up to that kid and hit him in the mouth as hard as you can, knock him out. He was not expecting that, and it was difficult for him to fight with a bloody nose. He was bigger and managed to get me on the ground once, but then our friend, Bo Bo Collins, had a German Sheppard named Apache, who jumped on the guy, tore his shirt off and pulled him off me. When we got up, the kid did not want to fight anymore, he went home.

Another time at Manual High School in Denver, Colorado, some of my fellow football jocks beat up a younger friend from our neighbourhood; I broke up the fight. They said to me, "if you don't watch out, you will be next." The next day I approached one of them alone, and said, "You said I would be next, okay, how about now?"

He went to remove his varsity jacket, and got his arms stuck in the sleeve; and that's when I hit him with a couple of straight lefts and a right; the fight was pretty much over after that. His cousins and friends wanted to retaliate at the park the next day; so I brought my brother, Gene Washington, James Grimes and Carl Hubbard. Their guys backed down; they knew they were no match. As we were walking away, one of the guys took a swing at me, I ducked, and then the fight was on. Several small fights broke out; I ended up physically stomping the guy I was fighting. Police were eventually called, and we all ended up scrambling.

One time, my sister Elouise talked Walter and I into going with her to a friend's party; it turned out to be Billy Madrow and the 24th St Motorcycle Gang. A fight broke out, and we soon found ourselves fighting angry bikers, back to back. It was kind of like a cartoon movie, "what on earth have we got ourselves into this time?" We barely made it out of there alive, and I learnt a valuable lesson that night; don't ever bite off more than you can chew. The next day, Walt said," ahh, it was nothing, just a few bumps and bruises, good thing they did not start shooting".

The 1960's was the flower power era, Woodstock, Hendricks, the Stones and Joplin. Most of the college kids had tried Pot or some psychedelic drugs. David Hilliard, a friend from Southern California, was a long hair hippy who loved to party, chase concurts and girls. Dave had connections, he was the rich kid on the block, his parents were well off, he did not have to work for a living, he already owned a Harley, and Coupe Deville. We worked the night shift at Samsonite Luggage in Montebello, a suburb of Denver. I enjoyed working the night shift, lots of good memories.

Raymond Lyle, David Hilliard and I went to several great rock concerts in Denver and Boulder, Colorado; Boulder was our best party place, I went to school there. We used to dress up for concerts with our head bands, one ear ring, beads, and big collar, flower shirt with bell bottom jeans; we thought we were so cool. Dave had many weed contacts; he could get the best deals, a kilo of Marijuana for only $300. Sometimes we would sell joints for $1 at concerts; you could get well over 1000 joints from a kilo.

Dave once talked me into taking some Orange Sunshine at a Red Rocks Amphil Theatre concert in Golden Colorado; featuring Janis Joplin and B.B King. Orange Sunshine was a psychedelic drug used in the 1960s by some college students and hippies to raise awareness and appreciation for music. The concert was great, the music and the light shows were magical, but when the concert was over, everything started moving in slow motion. The crowds of people leaving the stadium seemed like waves of water rippling over the ocean. I lost Dave in the crowd, and then found him later on the way to the car. I was sure glad to see him, because I suddenly had a feeling of doom; like I would never make it home that night. When I finally made it home, I was so relieved, but still feeling a bit anxious. Later that morning, I thought I died and went to heaven, then reborn; I could not sleep for 2 days after that.

My family was almost ready to have me committed; I was quoting scriptures at times, and said I was Jesus, that he lives in all of us. It took me at least a week to come down from that trip. I thought to myself one night that I'll never, never again, take anything that makes you lose touch with reality; that is not a good thing.

Young people under eighteen years of age should not drink, smoke or do illicit drugs. There is sufficient scientific evidence that supports the theory that no two brains respond the same; and chemical reactions could also affect people differently. To avoid serious consequences like addiction and other detrimental long term health affects; it is better for all young people to wait till they are twenty one to experiment with alcohol or drugs. Medical research has proven that certain areas of the human brain are not fully developed until age eighteen or twenty-one; including the cerebral cortex and other pleasure and pain centres.

I was drafted into the United States Army during my first year of college; I could have applied for a college deferment or hardship waiver because I had two other brothers serving in the military during the Vietnam era. I knew that the G.I. bill had many great benefits, like education and home loans, so I went; also I felt that to serve was my civic duty.

The Military was a great experience for me, and also many other young men. It was like a rite of passage to adulthood. There was not a lot of racial conflict between soldiers because everyone knew that the Military was racially diverse, and did not tolerate racial discrimination on any level. In the Military Services, everybody seems to get along; they respected each other, and there was an atmosphere of spree décor (pride in the military), unity, brotherhood, and working together as part of a team. The majority of soldiers drank beer or hard liquor at their base camps when off duty; while many went to the movie theatres, canteen or NCO club to unwind after a hard day at work.

Upon completion of military service, I went back to school. We bought a home in Montebello, 5301 Xanadu Street; a suburb of Denver. I transferred from Community College North Campus to a pre-law program at the University of Colorado in Boulder, Colorado. I studied constitutional law, court room procedures and international law.

I had to take a work study job at a law firm, Zarlengo Mott & Zarlengo; because the G.I. Bill was not enough at the time; only $300 monthly. My job was record keeping, filing court documents and serving subpoenas. There was a lot of drinking and partying going on with the partners. Being part Indian, I usually got drunk first, so I had to watch my drinking. On one occasion my girlfriend, Sarah Rundell, and I was celebrating a court case victory at one of the partners' home; I had too much to drink, fell leaving the house, and vaguely remembered the event the next day. On another occasion I got a DUI going home from a party; this was the last straw, I was forced to drop out of school for a while. I also knew about the Three Strike laws; one more DUI and I would be looking at a felony, with no chance for law school in the future.

I changed my major in college to Criminal Justice Management, and transferred to Metropolitan State College. I almost had enough credits to graduate with a bachelor of science, but I needed intern hours working in the field. I started working at the Denver Federal Building, as a Federal Corrections Officer Intern, and I also picked up extra hours as a volunteer Denver Juvenile Probation Officer. Most of the cases that I handled were minimum risk, the parolees and probationers were always on their best behaviour. Our clients were well aware that their probation officer could come around at any time. I have a Bachelor of Science from Metropolitan State College, Criminal Justice Management, Denver, Colorado.

We had lots of good times in Montebello; it was a place that all family members could all call home. I had a rose coloured Cadillac Eldorado we called the party mobile. I took a new job working at City Corp Financial Services, an investment lending company based out of New York. Myself and co-workers; Jean, Kathy, Lynn and Marilyn would go straight to happy hour after work on Friday nights. Those good old days came to an end after a failed relationship with an ex-girlfriend, Joyce Kneebone; who had a wonderful son named Christopher DeRay Kneebone. I had a few drinks one Saturday night, and went to the liquor store before it closed; the day next was football Sunday, and the liqueur stores are closed on Sunday. When I came home, the police were waiting, Joyce said, "I called them because you are not supposed to drink and drive". I can't emphasize enough, my older brother Luther died from cirrhosis of the liver, he drank almost daily. If you drink or smoke, please use moderation, just do it on weekends, let your body do its job and filter out the toxins. I finally decided to pack up and move to Seattle WA. I had heard a lot of good things about Seattle from close friends; I wanted a fresh start, to find new adventures, challenges and opportunities.

Chapter 9

Seattle, Washington

In 1988 I moved to Seattle, Washington, a beautiful state, lots of rain, green trees, blue lakes and snow-capped mountains. I previously researched the economy, job market and social event calendar online before deciding to move. There is always something exciting to do in Seattle, places to go, things to see. There are countless annual parades and fireworks events, Blue Angles, Bumper shoot, and the Bite of Seattle. Seattle is a leader in cultural diversity, and historically known for its wide range of culturally diverse communities and dining cuisines. Ballard is Scandinavian influenced, China Town is Chinese, Rainier Valley is Blacks, and the Central district is a mixture of all cultures. Seattle had its first black mayor, Norman Rice in, 1998, a great leader and strong supporter of minority and women businesses in Seattle.

Between 2004 and 2012, Seattle had a woman governor (Christine Gregoire) and two women U.S. Senators (Patty Murray and Maria Cantwell), all democrats, running the state. Seattle made great progress and had vast economic growth under their leadership. As the leader in computer technology, aviation and coffee shops, Seattle was also one of the first states in America to legalize marijuana, which created huge revenue for the state. In 2014, Ed Murray became the first openly gay Mayor in Seattle history.

My first apartment at 9th and Madison Street had a view of the Puget Sound, just walking distance from the waterfront, Pike Place Market and the Space Needle. I took the first job offer from the V.A. Hospital 1660 S. Columbian way, attended the University of Washington, received a BSN, and retired as a registered nurse. I met my first wife, Pam, while working at the V.A.; she had two small children Jamela and Derrick. We had some pretty good times when the kids were young; there were always the high school basketball, baseball and volleyball games to attend. We went to church every Sunday, but when the Kids grew up, our relationship fell apart, and we divorced in 2005.

In spring of 2005, I went to a friend's birthday party in Surrey, a suburb of Vancouver, Canada. After the party I rented a room in downtown Vancouver and met my current wife, Susan. She was partying with friends at a nightclub called It's a Secret. We went out to breakfast after the club closed, exchanged numbers and made another date for two weeks later. We commuted back and forth for a while, she would come stay one weekend with me and I would go stay with her the next weekend. I bought a home in Federal Way, Washington, and we got married one year later in 2006.

I am so very thankful to have had the opportunity to work with some of the most beautiful, understanding and compassionate people in the world; healthcare workers Dr Steven Steins, Elaine Detwiler and Frankie Manning of the V.A. Hospital were each very dedicated in bringing high quality nursing care to all our patients.

After retiring from the V.A. Hospital, I continued to work as an independent traveling contract nurse. Nursing is a very rewarding profession, helping the sick and injured on a daily basis is why we choose the profession. As a traveling nurse, I work Emergency rooms, intensive care and medical surgery units across the state, from Everett to Olympia, Washington. A few hospitals like Swedish, Tacoma General and Kindred, I have worked over two years at one time. Meeting and taking care of so many different people in the hospitals was very helpful in completion of this book; I was able to gain valuable insight into human nature. I heard many good stories about personal accomplishments, misfortunes, beliefs, and feelings on race relations; nurses are trained to be good listeners.

Chapter 10

Discrimination Continues

Today in America, the prison populations are still predominantly black. Blacks have the highest number of inmates on death row at any given time; and the reason is discrimination and lack of legal representation. Lack of employment opportunities forces some blacks to desperate measures to support their families. When human beings cannot adequately provide for their families, they feel like failures, and those feelings can cause depression and stress; which can put the entire family's health status at risk.

A lot of young black men ended up in the prison system, they found themselves with their backs against the wall; could not find adequate employment to support their families, so they turned to crime, and ended up doing hard time under the Three Strike Laws. Prejudices and separation between blacks and whites grew even more, because blacks stereotyped most whites as red neck racists, and whites stereotyped most blacks as criminals who can't hold down jobs.

Not all Presidential Administrations in history were openly supportive of the black struggle in America; a few had negative impacts on black progress and civil rights.

Some Administrations did not attempt to pass new civil rights legislation, and some Administrations repealed existing civil rights legislation. The Bush and Reagan Administrations did not reach out to the black community, nor did they pardon many blacks on death row in Texas or California when they were Governors and Presidents.

There was a federal case tried in Texas where a black man was dragged by the neck until decapitated by some white men in Texas when Bush was in office. It was a hate crime and the black community was outraged because the jury was lenient on the murderers, gave them short sentences and fines. Placing them on death row or Execution would have sent a strong message that hate crimes will not be tolerated in the United States. I am not saying that executions are good, but do you see a double standard? White hate groups like the KKK get jail time (if prosecuted) for murdering blacks; black groups like the Black Panthers, who constitutionally had a right to bear arms, protect and defend their properties, get executed. If you listen to the news, you can see that there is a double standard for sentencing in our justice system.

For those of you who think disparities and discrimination don't exist, look up National Healthcare Disparities Reports from 2005-2014. You will see that blacks are on the bottom of the healthcare scale. DHHS Secretary Tommy Thompson stated in 2005, "communities of colour suffer disproportionately from diabetes, heart disease, HIV/AIDS, cancer, stroke and infant mortality. Eliminating these and other health disparities is a priority of HHS." Public Law 106-129, the Healthcare Research and Quality (AHRQ) initiative developed two annual reports: a National Healthcare Quality Report (NHQR) and the National Healthcare Disparity Report (NHDR).The directive for the reports requires that it tracks "prevailing disparities in health care delivery as they relate to racial and socio-economic factors in priority populations."

The cost of healthcare coverage today keeps going up, this cost inflation has left many Americans without healthcare, and caused many to file bankruptcy, not just blacks and minorities, but poor white people as well. Healthcare should be free, universal for low income Americans, healthcare should be a privilege provided by the greatest nation on earth. It is a crime, an act of discrimination to deny blacks, minorities and poor people access to adequate healthcare, a basic human necessity. Big business, big insurance agencies, profit-driven physicians, and big pharmaceutical companies should be prosecuted by the Attorney General's office for discrimination based on income. The health and welfare of the general public is put at risk because they cannot afford basic healthcare, and the prices keep going up. America pays the most for healthcare than other developed nations in the world; it is the government's job to safeguard the health and welfare of Americans, not Insurance companies and lawyers who are profit motivated.

Free healthcare, like Civil Rights, are moral issues, and its opponents are greed, power and total disrespect for the basic needs of other human beings. The United States remains one of the wealthiest industrialized nations in the world without universal healthcare. In 1993, President Bill Clinton formed a task force on healthcare reforms to provide comprehensive healthcare to all Americans, the chair of the task force was the first lady, Hillary Rodham Clinton. The Surgeon General C. Everett Koop supported the administrations universal healthcare reform efforts and the proposed Health Security Act to bring healthcare to millions of unemployed Americans, and to require employers to assist in providing healthcare coverage for under insured employees. Opposition to the plan came from conservatives, libertarians, health insurance agencies, and groups like the Project for the Republican Future. Scare tactics were used to confuse the public, just like opponents are trying to do today to kill President Obama's health care reform legislation. The opponents in 1993 used deceptive television advertisements like Harry and Louise, a middle class couple who was in despair over the complexity of the proposed plan; just like today, opponents are saying that the current plan will cut Medicare benefits, kill granny by pulling the plug when she is elderly and ill to cut medical expenses. Opponents today are saying we don't have a healthcare problem, just like in 1993, Senator Daniel Patrick Moynihan argued that we do not have a healthcare crisis in America, just an insurance problem than can work if government keep their hands off. Who are the people against universal healthcare? The very rich, the big businesses, big drug companies, big insurance companies, and employers who do not want to pay for their employee's healthcare. Why are they against the plan? Because they don't mind if healthcare costs continue to rise, they want to make a profit for themselves, with no concerns for the billions of Americans without healthcare insurance, it is called UN –American.

Look at the Three Strikes laws enacted in the 1980's, they were designed to keep violent offenders off the streets, to keep society safe; but in reality, these laws only increased discrimination against the poor. They became a tool to discriminate against blacks and other minorities. Many blacks were charged under the Three Strikes laws for petty offenses, like disturbance, domestic violence, theft, possession of marijuana, while many of the white-collar, hard-core criminals, who committed bank fraud, illegal gambling, internet scams, predatory banking, tax evasion, organized insurance scams and other acts of fraud could afford legal representation. Plea bargaining by lawyers in court was a legal strategy to avoid the Three Strike laws, and reduce your sentence. Many of those blacks and other minorities charged under the Three Strike laws who did not have property (property which was systematically stolen from their parents), could not raise the bail, or pay attorney fees, they were charged with three strikes and sentenced to unjust, lengthy terms of incarceration.

Laws that discriminate against blacks need to be declared unconstitutional, laws like Three Strikes, and Stand your Own Ground. Why is it that most ethnic and racial groups in America who were treated unfairly in the past were compensated by the Federal Government, except black people? The Japanese Americans, who were held in detainment camps during World War I, were compensated with land and money. The American Indians are still being compensated by free land, money, homes and casinos, all provided by the Federal Government. In Washington State, the government just built a 40 million dollar casino on the Snoqualmie Indian Reservation, the money was a federal loan; the casinos make huge profits, and employees, get big bonuses.

Affirmative action was a provision of the 1972 Equal Employment Opportunities act, meant to correct the problems of discrimination in hiring and employment practices. It was challenged in 1978, Regents of the University of California v. Bakke, the legal precedent for challenging affirmative action based on the theory of reverse discrimination was established. What were the justices thinking? Affirmative action was designed to reverse discrimination, theoretically you cannot reverse an object in motion without bringing it to a stop first, and discrimination in employment had not stopped in America. There are many people who think that we are all equal in America, and we should do away with affirmative action. I say to them, just take a look at any national or state unemployment census.

Chapter 11

U.S. Presidents, Slavery and Civil Rights

It takes a very special and gifted individual to be President of the United States, head of state and government, commander in chief to the United States Armed Forces, with executive powers to sign treaties, declare war, grant pardons, pass and veto new legislation. The President of the United States historically has had a tremendous impact on the black struggle. The single most powerful man in America, as our nation's leader, the President can influence the way the country feels about human rights, policy making, and the legal system. We as Americans are very fortunate and blessed for all the great presidents we have had throughout history. The majority of the first 15 Presidents shared common moral values that slavery was wrong, but was met with opposition when trying to pass legislation by a predominantly pro-slavery democratic and republican influenced congress; some of whom owned slaves. The wealthy land owners and farmers were against freedom for slaves because of greed and profits they would lose if they had to pay people to work their farms and plantations. The 16th President Abraham Lincoln ignored the advice of his cabinet and congress by ending slavery at the end of the civil war, by making an Emancipation Proclamation.

George Washington, the first President from 1789-1797, was a slave owner, cotton, tobacco and hemp farmer who changed his views on slavery once he became president. George Washington was a farmer and plantation owner who had many slaves, was against slavery while in office, and freed many of his slaves in his will to be effective, after his death and the death of his wife Martha. There are rumours that George Washington fathered a black child; the child's name was West Ford, son of a slave woman by the name of Venus from his brother's plantation. John Adams, President from 1779-1801, Vice President to George Washington, denounced slavery, supported legislation to end slavery, but did very little to change the system. President Adams did not want to divide the country on the issue of slavery, keeping the union together was his main priority. Thomas Jefferson, President from 1801-1809, was a slave owner, cotton, tobacco and hemp farmer, who wrote the Declaration of Independence, had a clause in it denouncing slavery, but the congress rejected that section. Jefferson was said to have taken a slave, Sally Hemings, as a concubine. She had four children, Beverly, Harriet, Madison, and Eston. Jefferson did not want to tackle the slavery issue because congress convinced him it would lead to a revolution. Jefferson freed all his slave children on their 21st birthday. Most of the last 37 presidents starting with President Abraham Lincoln, shared a common interest in freedom and civil rights for all Americans, a few took the pro southern position.

Abraham Lincoln, President from 1861-1865, opponent of slavery, country lawyer from Illinois and member of the U.S. House of Representatives, Lincoln issued his historic Emancipation Proclamation on January 1, 1863, abolishing slavery in the United States, and encouraged the passage of the Thirteenth Amendment, a constitutional law forbidding slavery. Like past presidents, Lincoln was encouraged by members of congress to hold off on emancipation the slaves, this would divide the nation, but Lincoln knew this was the right time, the reason for fighting the civil War, civil rights for all Americans. To end the Civil War, Lincoln needed additional troops, he was reported as saying "why must we fight with one hand tied behind our backs, untie our other hand and let the black man fight for his freedom." He initiated the first U.S. Draft, enlisted black soldiers, formed all black units which were courageous in battle, legends were written about the courageous buffalo soldiers who fought to the death, they made the difference and forced the surrender of the confederate army.

Andrew Johnson, President from 1865-1869; was against civil rights, he vetoed the Civil Rights Act of 1866, which gave blacks the right to own property, make contracts, sue and bear witness against white people in a court of law. Johnson was in favour of the black codes of the south, against everything that the Civil War and Lincoln accomplished for blacks. Johnson believed that blacks were not qualified for citizenship, and the bill would work in favour of blacks and against white people. Fortunate for America the congress overrode the presidential veto, stating that blacks were citizens.

Ulysses S. Grant, President from 1869-1877; Grant was a strong supporter of civil rights and the Lincoln policies; he fought against Andrew Johnson's laws and policies. As Commanding General of the United States Army, during Abraham Lincoln's presidency, Grant forced the surrender of General Robert E. Lee 1865, ending the civil war. President Grant enforced civil rights legislation, and fought for passage of the Fifteenth Amendment 1870, prohibited government from denying citizens the right to vote based on race or x-slave status.

Franklin D. Roosevelt, president from 1933-1945; the only president to serve 4 terms in office and one of eight to die to office; Lincoln, Garfield, McKinley and Kennedy were assassinated. FDR was a great president in many ways; he led the country through the great depression and declared war against Japan in WWII. FDR let black America down, in order to pass his new deal legislation to put Americans back to work during the depression, he choose not to sign any anti-lynching laws because he was threatened with a filibuster from special interest group who controlled congress. According to an Internet article, Franklin D. Roosevelt assumed the presidency of a nation in which white supremacy was a significant cultural and political force. Many states denied or severely restricted voting rights to African Americans and used their political power to further diminish their status and to deny them the benefits and opportunities of society. One consequence of this was to make a kind of "people's justice,' in which mobs of whites seized and murdered, often in gruesome fashion, African Americans suspected of crimes against whites. The article went on to say that FDR gave somewhat of an apology to the NAACP and black people, stating that he did not choose the tools he had to work with, and in 1941 FDR issued Executive order 8802 to create the Fair Employment Practice Committee. The president overlooked the most important aspect of civil right, the right to life, he fell victim to the pressures of special interest groups, but his wife, Eleanor, on the other hand, stood up for equal rights and racial justice. FDR could have prevented years of suffering and intimidation of blacks by white mobs in the south by eliminating the lynching laws; blacks would have stood up for their civil rights and protested for the right to vote, and for equal employment rights. Lynching continued to be a tool of white supremacy until the civil rights movements of the 1960's, Martin Luther King and John F. Kennedy were instrumental factors in ending lynching in America.

Harry S. Truman, President from 1945-1953, was mostly remembered for his decision to use the atomic bomb against Japan in WWII. Truman was a strong supporter of civil rights during his presidency, he encouraged his administration to fight for desegregation through the south, and he made an executive order to desegregate the military services, mandating that equal opportunity be provided in all military branches of service and in all federal agencies, regardless of race or the colour of a person's skin. The executive order was very important in history, because it was at a time when white supremacy beliefs were that economic and legal discrimination against non-whites were justified. Dwight D. Eisenhower, President from 1953-1962; Supreme Commander of NATO during World War II, as President passed the first civil rights legislation, the Civil Rights Act of 1957, and voting rights legislation of 1960. Eisenhower enforced the Truman executive order to desegregate the military services, he sent the 101st Airborne Division to Arkansas to support integration of public schools, and was the first president to meet with civil rights leaders at the White House. Eisenhower has one of the highest approval ratings of U.S. Presidents.

John F. Kennedy, President from 1961-1963; senator from Massachusetts, known for foreign policy and the cold war, he was tough on the Soviet Union, not allowing missiles in Cuba, a key figure in developing the Civil Rights Act of 1964. There were racial uprisings in the south; Martin L. King and Meagre Evers were organizing demonstrations, blacks were still being lynched, not allowed to ride in the front of busses or register to vote. In his inaugural address in 1962, Kennedy promised to end racial discrimination, in response Kennedy said new Civil Rights legislation need to be passed, it is a "moral issue, it is as old as the scriptures and is as clear as the American Constitution." Kennedy stated that, "Lincoln freed the slaves 100 years ago, and still black people are not free, the law forbids discrimination in public schools in Brown v. Board of Education, but still many schools are not integrated, the 14th Amendment guarantees equal protection under the law, yet there are places where blacks cannot eat in a public restaurant". The new civil rights laws he proposed involved rights to vote, go to school, get a job and be served in a public place. Kennedy enforced the equal protection law by sending federal troops to the University of Alabama, where governor George Wallace forbid black students from entering the school. Enforcement of the equal protection guarantee of the 14th Amendment was the beginning of the end of lynching in America, because southerners realized that they could be federally prosecuted. President Kennedy was assassinated in Texas before the civil rights act was approved by Congress. President JFK's legacy and popularity was magnified by his family's accomplishments, civil rights activists themselves; his father, Joseph Kennedy, an influential political leader and Ambassador, his brothers Robert and Edward, U.S. Senators; Robert F. Kenney(RFK) was also Attorney General, a civil rights activist, who worked with Dr. Martin Luther King, helped release him from jail for peaceful demonstrations in the south and fought against Edgar Hoover (FBI Director), who did not like King and wire tapped his phones, offices, and called him a communist.

Richard M. Nixon, President 1969-1974; was a lawyer, officer in the Navy, a Senator from California, and Vice President to Dwight D. Eisenhower in 1952. Nixon is most remembered for his role in the Vietnam War, and the only President to resign office, due to the Watergate Conspiracy. What many people don't know is that he was for universal healthcare; he wanted to provide health insurance for all Americans. Nixon's Comprehensive Health Insurance Act proposed at his 1974 State of the Union address, "I shall propose a sweeping new program that will assure comprehensive health insurance protection to millions of Americans who cannot now obtain it or afford it, with vastly improved protection against catastrophic illnesses." Nixon teamed up with Senator Edward Kennedy to write the bill, but it was not completed because Watergate happened, and he was forced to resign, then congress killed the bill. The Republican Party turned their backs on Nixon during Watergate, because big businesses, and big insurance companies, profit-motivated doctors and lawyers did not want this bill passed, they did not want to pay for catastrophic illnesses or multi system failures like cancer; the way they make a profit is to deny as many claims as possible.

Jimmy Carter, President from 1977-1981, was a strong supporter of human rights and democracy, a religious man, educated in technology, and graduate from the U.S Naval Academy. Carter was a democrat who believed in non-partisan legislation. As President, he introduced two pieces of legislation, the Hospital Cost Containment Act of 1977, and the Child Health Assessment Program (CHAP); both were met with strong opposition by congress. The main reason for the failure was that there was a provision for a national health insurance program, just like single payer or public option which would provide choice to the American public and competition for insurance agencies. The big insurance agencies would lose some control over pricing, if people had a choice; they were not going for that, the insurance agencies paid out millions to defeat this bill. The Hospital Containment Act would have provided a national health insurance program, controlled wage increases for hospital business executives, and cut down on unnecessary hospitalizations and procedures which were profit motivated. "For the federal budget, rising health spending has meant a tripling of health outlays over the last eight years. Without immediate action, the Federal government's bill for Medicare and Medicaid,-which provides health care for our elderly and poor citizens, will jump nearly 23 percent next year to $32 billion." Carter went on to say that "Rising health costs attack state and local governments as well. State and local Medicaid expenditures have grown from $3 billion in 1971 to $7 billion in 1976, forcing cutbacks which harm the low income recipients of the program." The Child Health Assessment Program was written to extend benefits to children who did not meet state eligibility, and assure health providers for low income children. "Currently, twelve million children are eligible for Medicaid, yet the EPSDT program is reaching only two million. Further, only slightly more than half of all children screened actually receive treatment for conditions that are identified. The CHAP program will assist the states in rectifying these deficiencies." Carter's legislation was defeated by congress, and new proposals were written which favour big businesses and insurance agencies, the same old objections were that business runs better without government interventions. The next President, Ronald Reagan was for big business and tax cuts to the wealthiest of Americans, so he killed the Carter initiatives dead in their tracks.

Ronald Reagan, President from 1981-1989, was an actor turned politician. As president, he implemented Reaganomics, supply-side economics, with reduced business regulations, reduced government spending on social programs, gave big tax cuts to wealthy Americans and big businesses. Reagan brought down inflation, because consumers did not have money to spend, and he was instrumental in ending the cold war with Russia, whose economy was collapsing already because of the United States cut backs on oil purchases. Ronald Reagan was not a strong supporter of civil rights, and was against Medicaid and Medicare for the poor. In 1976, Reagan ran against incumbent President Gerald Ford, to win the Southern vote. Reagan took sides with Barry Goldwater, supporting the

Southern views on Civil Rights and Affirmative Action; he believed that each state should have control over enforcing their own laws. Southern politicians called the Civil Rights Act an attack on "the Southern way of life." Reagan accused Ford of supporting forced integration in the south.

William J. Clinton, President from 1993-2001, was a Rhodes Scholar, Law professor at University of Arkansas, and two term governor of Arkansas. He met his wife Hillary Rodham while studying law at Yale. The Clinton administration was dedicated to equality, justice and civil rights; there was a commission on race and the holocaust, councils on healthcare, welfare reforms and women rights. The Clinton administration fought to bring about universal healthcare for all Americans, but the plan was defeated by republicans in Congress, big business and greed. In his inaugural address, William J. Clinton stated that, "Americans deserve better, and in this city today there are people who want to do better, and so I say to all of you here, let us resolve to reform our politics, so that power and privilege no longer shout down the voice of the people." Clinton was aware of the historical 'good old boys' privileged groups who fought with past presidents to prevent freedom and civil rights for a nation of American black and minority citizens. During Clintons administration, several federal initiatives addressing racial and health disparities were launched; Healthy People 2010, Racial and Ethnic Approaches to Community Health (REACH) and Excellence Centre to Eliminate Ethnic/Racial Disparities (EXCEED). Hillary Clinton played a major role in healthcare reforms of the administration. Bill Clinton once commented that Thomas Jefferson wrote the Declaration of Independence in 1776, which freed the slaves, but work still need to be done to ensure the rights and privileges of American citizens; the Fourteenth Amendment guarantees equal protection under the law for citizens of the United States, but the laws are not being enforced in every state. Clinton made a public apology during his Presidency to black people for the ethical and moral misconduct of the Tuskegee Syphilis Studies.

Chapter 12

The First Black American President

During the Presidential elections of November of 2008, as the election results rolled in, it showed Senator Barack Obama as the clear choice of the American people from start to finish; he never trailed. This was a time of true joy and jubilation; America was ecstatic, especially the black community. The whole world was witnessing history being made; let music play, and the celebration begin. This was an event of monumental significance for black people, it represented self-actualization as a race; an event that every black person has dreamed about their entire life; and many people thought they would never see.

The National Anthem was being played on National Television; there were fireworks everywhere, car horns blowing around the city, people out in the streets cheering. There were famous celebrities on national news stations crying with joy; phone lines were jammed everywhere with local and international calls coming in and going out. When I finally got through to my mother, we said a prayer for our grandfather and the others who never lived to see this day. Many of our black fathers and mothers can relate to family discussions and thought that they would never see a black President in the United States of America. Americans were celebrating in the streets in every state, like a major holiday, the fourth of July; many people did not go to work the next day. America had just hit the lottery, won the super bowl and World Series in one night; it was a good time to be an American.

Many white people were happy with the elections because everybody knew we elected a qualified person for the job, a person with leadership ambitions, experience that the nation desperately needed. Senator Barack Obama was just what the country needed, as President; he has the knowledge, power and leadership experience to bring the country together on major issues confronting the nation. The people were ready for a change in Washington, the current administration left the country in war, and a huge financial deficit. To get this country rolling, President Barack would rely of his experience as a Harvard law graduate and community organizer to unite America in common goals to improve the quality of life for all Americans.

As the first months rolled on in 2009 with the Obama administration, he proved true to his campaign promise of bipartisan legislation by nominating republicans to his cabinet. Obama tried to use bipartisan legislation to get an economic stimulus package passed through congress, and cash for clunkers program to boost sales for the failing auto industry, in an effort to get this country back on the road to recovery. Both efforts were very successful, but opposed by republican members of congress all the way. Obama was true to his campaign promise of ending the war in Iraq by meeting with his cabinet and military leaders to decide the best way start troop withdrawals, but his efforts once again are opposed by republicans. Obama accomplished what few other Presidents were able to do, open a dialog of improved foreign policy with China, Cuba, Afghanistan and Pakistan.

On healthcare legislation, he chose a soft approach, unlike his predecessors, asking tor unrestricted free health care; Obama proposed a public option plan to bring healthcare to millions with no coverage and strengthened efforts to decrease the cost of healthcare for millions of others. The health insurance plan proposed by President Obama was opposed by republicans and private healthcare insurers because this plan would put a cap on runaway healthcare costs, prevent companies from denying pre-existing medical claims, and force private insurers to lower prices or go out of business. The healthcare industry today is profit motivated, and it should be patient care motivated. The drug companies use tax payers' dollars for research, and then raise the prices for marketing and executive bonuses. Healthcare is a basic human need; it is discrimination for low income Americans, blacks and other minorities to be denied that basic human need. It is Incomprehensible to me that 10-20% of Americans may have adequate healthcare coverage, while the other 80-90% does not have adequate healthcare coverage.

Many people feel that the strong opposition to Obama's administration was racially motivated; past Presidents Jimmy Carter and Bill Clinton commented on national television that the manner in which the southern members of Congress are reacting to the President, showing a lack of respect for the head of state and federal government, show signs of racial prejudice. Obama denied the allegations; he believes that the motivations are political, based on policy and healthcare issues, greed and profit for a small group of Americans, at the expense of the vast majority.

During his first year in office, Obama took control of a sinking ship, and started bailing water, putting America back on its feet again. President Obama has done what no other President in history has ever done; he took a large amount of money, over $700 billion, from the Federal Reserve and gave millions directly to the American people in need, when they were losing their jobs and homes in a failing economy, passed major health care reforms, and also won the Nobel Peace Prize for his humanitarian efforts. The first recovery package proposed by the president was initially written to give more money per individual and family households than allowed by opponents of the bill. Americans felt pride for the first time that our government actually cared for the welfare of its citizens. Obama made great progress in reaching out to the international community, he develops better diplomatic relations, opened a dialogue with the United Nations for negotiations on nuclear arms disarmament, arms control, and climate change. The Norwegian Nobel Committee decided that the 2009 Nobel Peace Prize should go to President Barack Obama for his great accomplishments and extraordinary efforts to promote peace and international diplomacy.

The election of a Republican Senator, Scott Brown to the Massachusetts senate seat vacated in 2010 by the death of Senator Edward Kennedy; republicans had enough votes to filibuster the healthcare reform bills. A filibuster is a Senate rule requiring two thirds majority vote to pass a bill in the Senate. For God's sake, whose side is the Republican and Blue Dog Democrats on? If you voted for a Senator or congressman or woman who voted against healthcare reforms and the public option, you are just as guilty as they are, you should be ashamed and held accountable for their actions. In the eyes of God, this is wrong, to deny healthcare to Americans without health insurance, who cannot afford basic health maintenance. The lowest healthcare plans available starts at $500.00 per family member monthly, which is not ethical when the economy is bad, and many people lost their jobs.

According to a recent article on US Politics, "The filibuster is a historical method used to delay vote or block debate in the senate. Some call it unconstitutional, unfair, and a historical relic. Others insist that it is a tool that protects the rights of the minority against the tyranny of the majority."

The article went on to say, "the word filibuster derived from the Dutch work meaning "pirate" was first used more than 150 years ago to describe 'efforts to hold the Senate floor in order to prevent action on a bill.'" Excuse me, why are we protecting the rights of the minority senators who work for special interest groups? The majority of senators are working for the people, and voted for healthcare reforms. We the people chose our system of government as a Democracy, not a Corporatism, Communist or Confederation. In a Democracy, the majority rules, the power belongs to the people, and the people have spoken: we do not want to delay action on health care reforms, we need it now. According to that same article, the filibuster has been used many times in the past to block historical civil rights legislation. In 1957; Strom Thurmond of South Carolina set a filibuster record to block the Civil Rights Act of 1957, and again in 1964 by Robert Byrd of West Virginia in an unsuccessful attempt to block the Civil Rights Act of 1964. Special interest rules in our political system should be declared obsolete and unconstitutional by the President of the United States, better yet he should use his executive power to make a health emancipation proclamation, that healthcare is basic human rights, and should be free for all Americans.

In his 2010 State of the Union Address, President Obama had not given up on health care reform, there is still work to be done, the president has other priorities as well, like job creation, helping the banks stay afloat to give loans to small businesses to hire workers, and put Americans back to work. Keeping Americans from losing their homes, controlling the economy and bringing down the national federal deficit, which doubled during the Bush Administration; national spending was out of control when Obama took office, spending on war efforts cost the country billions. President Obama voiced his disappointment in the Supreme Court for supporting a decision to allow special interest groups to control politics in America. The Election committee doesn't care where candidates get their money from, which is wrong, national interest should be the main concern. Campaign contributions could come from the KKK, the Soviet Union or the Taliban; they don't care, but we need to consider the interest of the American people.

In his 2011 State of the Union Address, President Obama still has not given up on a comprehensive health care plan, but faces many new challenges with the now divided congress. The Senate has a democratic majority, while the House has a republican majority and the speaker, John Boehner from Ohio, stood by quietly and let republican congressmen members insult the President of the United States of America on national television. A true leader would have called them out for that; he sold out to the highest bidder. Historically, when there is a divided in congress, it is difficult to pass new legislation that both the House and Senate can agree on; but now, more than ever, because republicans in congress has only one agenda, that is to ensure that the Obama administration fails. John Boehner and the republicans have vowed to repeal the new healthcare laws that president Obama has worked hard to pass. Insurance companies should not be allowed to raise prices at will, and cancel policies for pre-existing conditions. It is apparent that republicans are not willing to compromise, and put their differences aside for the health and welfare for the American people.

The President wants America to take responsibility for the nation's deficits by freezing domestic spending; which is a good thing, because here we are in debt, but giving billions of dollars in aid to other countries, we need to stop policing the world when Americans are unemployed and losing their homes. The President wants to eliminate tax breaks for oil companies, and companies that open factories in other countries to save on labour cost; we need the jobs in America. The President wants to tax the wealthiest Americans more than the poor; which is a good thing because the rich made their wealth off the average American consumers buying their products, who now need their help and support; but they turn their backs on us, are we not our brother's keepers. Why would wealthy Americans feel that everyone should be taxed equally? Because of self-interest, call it greed, profit; so un-American.

In his 2012 State of the Union Address, the President wants to continue to bring troops home from around the world. He wants to restore the economy back to where everyone gets a fair share, by having the wealthiest Americans pay their fair share of taxes, by eliminating tax breaks to the rich from the previous administration, and by eliminating tax breaks to big companies who open factories overseas, we need more jobs in America. The president came face to face with special interest group greed and corruption. Many Americans felt that the Republican candidate for President, Mick Romney, supported the rich and powerful special interest groups in America. The needs of the average American were not one of his main priorities; he would have made the rich richer and the poor poorer.

In his 2013 State of the Union Address, the President is holding the course, not changing from his original vision for America, he wants everyone to share in the American dream, and he wants to preserve social security, increase minimum wages and keep education affordable.

In his 2014 State of the Union Address, the President is still committed to improving the quality of life for all Americans, making government work more efficiently, education for our children, keeping Americans safe, bringing more military troops home from abroad, and unifying Americans to common goals.

We can start to see some change in our country, personal and institutional changes in the way the country feels about discrimination, it is not a popular thing to do anymore, and you would be charged with a crime, not like in the old days when the law would not prosecute discrimination offences. When you have a black person, minority or woman in a high legislative position of authority, the negative stereotyping starts to evaporate; no longer can anyone say blacks or women are not qualified for certain positions. Parents cannot teach their children that blacks, minorities and women are not intellectually qualified for high positions of authority, because now they can see the truth.

The younger generation of Americans can see with their own eyes that negative stereotyping of people is wrong, based on myths, and that attitudes of prejudices are starting to become a thing of the past in America. Let's just be Americans first and get rid of ethnic labels, racial divisions of black, and white, Asian or Indian. We are all aware of the melting pot theories, ethnic and cultural blending of America. There is a new breed of Americans evolving who are of mixed races, who do not identify with one race, who just consider themselves Americans.

The legacy of the first black American president will go down in history as one of the greatest American triumphs for humanity and equality. Obama was able to be elected to and complete two turns in office as the President of the United States of America during very difficult times when the economy was struggling, government shutdowns, and morality was low and many Americans lack faith in our countries political leadership abilities. He was able to unite Americans, young and old, black and white, rich and poor to a common goal; and that is what makes America a better place for all Americans.

The President has satisfied the hearts of Black America, he gave them a greater sense value and pride, in reality psychosocially, black people as a race can move forward, take a step closer to fulfilling a basic human need, self-actuation, the ability to be all you can be, because the doors are open.

For the many of our Black American forefathers and mothers who dreamed about the day a black man would be President, but never got to see that dream come true; let your wandering souls reach out from the depths of purgatory, rejoice, rest in peace; behold the first Black American President of the United States of America is history now. This President will hold true to the fulfilment of Dr. Martin Luther King's dream; the same dream of black people since the beginning of slavery.

President Barack Obama is a true humanitarian, just like Abraham Lincoln and Martin Luther King, they stand for justice and equality, they challenge America to move forward and be the great nation it has aspired to be from its beginning; a nation of freedom and liberty for all. As we near the end of Barrack's second term in office, I don't think we heard the last from Barrack and Michelle Obama on the political scene.

Many people can remember the 1950's and 1960's, in public school, standing at attention during the first hour of classes, where ever you were, on the steps, standing in the hallways, on the playground; we pledged the allegiance to the flag of the United States of America, one nation under God, indivisible with liberty and justice for all.

Chapter 13

Even the Baseball Field

In 2008, the election of Barrack Obama as the first African American President in the history of the United States was like a holiday celebration, the fourth of July, the feeling you get when your hometown sports team wins the super bowl or world series; people were out in the streets celebrating. This election changed many views on American politics, attitudes and perceptions of cultural and racial relationships. The Three Strikes paradigm has just improved for the black man in America; change for the better of all mankind is in progress. People everywhere were noticing a changed in attitudes overnight. Strangers started loving one another, being friendlier to each other, reaching out to socialize with other cultural and racial groups for the first time.

The problems with equality on the baseball fields of life exist today because of past discriminatory practices and customs which created racial disparities in America. There are many non-blacks, and the younger generation of Americans born after 1970; that are not aware that systematic racial barriers and discrimination still exist in America today.

Many non-black Americans can't understand how blacks can be disadvantaged economically today when many blacks play major league sports, but just consider the ratio of white to black coaches, owners, politicians and millionaires. Yes, there are a few wealthy blacks in America today, but the percentage is small compared to all Americans; take a look at the Forbes Wealthy American list, less than five percent are black. The wealthiest people made their fortune from inheritance, real estate, oil production, banking or private businesses, like Microsoft or Google. Most blacks never had the real estate, financial collateral to build the small business or bank; remember that many black had their land and property stolen from them years ago.

My mother commented that we have a long way to go to level the field, putting God, family and country first is important. Maintaining a strong family structure helps build economic wealth and support for family members. When strangers put you in chains, steal your freedom, sell your uncles, brothers and sisters on auction blocks, and you never see them again, this puts your whole family at a disadvantage in social and economic wealth.

A lot of young black men ended up in the prison system, they found themselves with their backs against the wall, could not find adequate employment to support their families, so they turn to crime. When you are black, once you get a criminal record, most employers will not even consider your job application, even if you were wrongfully charged. Racial profiling must be abolished forever; we don't ever want to have another incidence like the Boston Mass. Willy Green violations of human rights happen again in America. There was a criminal investigation in Boston 1960's, a prominent white Doctor killed his wife and said a black man did it. The City was outraged, so the police violated the constitutional rights of many African American males; arrested them on the street and in their homes without probable cause or warrants, just because they were black, and the police wanted answers. The Doctor later confessed to the murders, but don't you see the damage is done; they have ruined the lives of those young men for something they did not do.

To achieve equality, all black and minority children should be educated; they should be given the opportunity to attend any school of choice. Bring back the affirmative action programs of the 1960's, which provided education, social health and human services programs designed to help deprived minorities youth. Many white kids in the past have had the advantages and opportunities to attend the best schools, like Yale, Harvard and Duke; more doors need to be opened for black children to get better educations.

We need more educational opportunities for all Americans, and maybe if blacks and minorities had more educational opportunities and equal access to private business ownerships, minorities would not have to work so hard on physical labour like sports and music to succeed; but use their minds to cure cancer, eliminate hunger and war.

Like the game of baseball, you are supposed to get three strikes at bat, but because of your colour, you are disadvantaged, you only get one strike; baseball, football or basketball may be your only way out of the ghetto, and you have to hit a home run the first strike. As a black male, you know that the cards are stacked against you, and you won't get a second chance. You have to go out and make the money to support your family. Fifty acre and a mule promised poor black slaves was that just another blank check, broken promise to keep them quiet. We need to cash in on those blank checks, and demand from our government equal protection and universal healthcare.

In present times, 2014, we have a black president working for the common good of all Americans. It's hard to be bitter over the past, and easy to be forgiving of past injustices and inequalities historically done to black people. This generation of children in America grew up integrated; black and white, brown and yellow children together in almost every school in the United States. Let's work to improve the quality of life for all Americans.

Americans have always aspired to be Christians and true Humanitarians, they understand right from wrong, and most Americans would like to correct the damage done through past discriminatory practices. Nature and evolution has a way of correcting its own problems, over time; the problems of human socialization would also correct themselves if there were not so many barriers, manmade obstacles to disrupt this process. If you study statistics, laws of averages say that sooner or later the underdog will rise to the top, and then find stability; we will all average out to be equal in the end. It's human nature for all of us to cheer for the underdog in any competition. Like random numbers, now the ones on top will someday be the ones on the bottom, and the ones on the bottom will have to work harder to get back on top.

The 'good old boy' days of privileged groups in America are coming to an end. White male domination in government and private business is levelling out. We are starting to see more minority and women political leaders emerging; leaders with integrity, like Barrack Obama, and Hillary Clinton. We, as Americans, can start to enjoy the benefits and rewards of life as true humanitarians; and set the example for other countries like, England, Canada, and France.

As Americans, we must return to our roots, put the church first, and recapture our national pride and morality. The church is the foundation of American unity; Life, Liberty and the pursuit of happiness for all God's creations. We don't need international conflicts and war, what we need is universal love and understanding. Come on,

America, let's do the right thing, let us inspire a shared vision to the world of international love and peace.

We, as Americans, should be proud, unite and start rebuilding bridges for better human relations. Let's not dwell on injustices of the past, but move forward in harmony as a nation with a common goal. Let's learn from our mistakes, and be proactive humanitarians. Take the civil war, when the Confederate General Robert E. Lee surrendered to Union General Ulysses S. Grant in 1865; Grant showed kindness and compassion by letting Lee's men keep most of their possessions and return home to families, free to go. Grant showed kindness and compassion by enforcing civil rights legislation and fighting the KKK during his presidency. We should all show kindness and compassion, not only to our enemies, but fellow Americans as well.

THE LORD'S PRAYER

Our father who art in heaven, hallowed be thy name.Thy kingdom come. Thy will be done on earth as it is in heaven. Give us this day our daily bread, and forgive us our trespasses, as we forgive those who trespass against us, but lead us not into temptation, but deliver us from evil, for thou is the kingdom, the power and the glory forever, Amen. (Matthew 6:9-13).

Chapter 14

Comments from Family and Friends

My mother, Frances L Williams, who was born in Arkansas, and later lived in Denver, CO, stated that we still have a long way to go to make up for all the injustices of the past. Things in the south are getting better; the younger generations of children who attended integrated schools are making the difference, they know other kids as friends; regardless of the colour of their skin, they respect each other for who they are not what they are. I think that President Obama is doing a great job in the White House; his critics just need to back off and give him time to bring about change. Franklin D. Roosevelt was credited with bringing America out of the 1950's depression, Barrack Obama is capable of doing the same for the economy today, and he just needs time to clean up the damage and corruption left by previous administrations. I think that Michelle Obama is going to be a great First Lady; through history, First Ladies have played significant roles in the black struggle for equality. Eleanor Roosevelt insisted on a black opera singer, Marian Anderson, to sing at the Lincoln Memorial Easter Sunday April 9, 1939 in Washington D.C., which was forbidden in those days. This opened up the door for many black singers to appear in major

Broadway theatres around the country. Hillary R. Clinton reached out to and brought national attention to the needs of black children and their struggle for equality and justice in America, and Africa.

My wife, Susan M. Schnarr-Williams, stated that "discrimination is becoming a thing of the past, and there were a lot of good white people who fought against discrimination in the past. Many white people went along with racism and discrimination because of fear that hate organizations like the KKK would come after them if they stood up against racism."

My brother, Walter H Williams, who lives in Denver, CO, stated that "systemic discrimination of minorities exists all over the world, not just in America, even in our military services abroad. It's going to take time to change all the old discriminatory practices". Walter said, "The Presidents overall rating as an American President, on a scale of one to ten, I would give him a ten. I think Obama has done a great job as leader and President; but as far as the black struggle is concerned, I would not put him in the same category with Abraham Lincoln, Martin L. King and John F. Kennedy".

My sister, Elouise Davis of Fordyce, Arkansas, stated, "The President is still trying to repair the damage left by the previous administration; he is doing a great job with Foreign Policy, he brought the troops home, and he works for the betterment of all people; not just Americans. White people are still prejudiced in Fordyce, they don't openly discriminate anymore, but they are sly, try to hide their true feelings with fake smiles and hellos."

My sister, Paulette McIntosh of Denver, Colorado, agrees with most people that President Obama is doing a good job. "On a scale of one to ten, I would give the President an eight because of the grid lock and opposition he faced from a Republican House. I believe the President's legacy will be his transparency to the American people; his energy, openness, and honesties were apparent to everyone around the world. His goal has always been to make America a better place for everyone".

My brother, Steven Williams of Phoenix, Arizona, stated that, "although the President had to face a lot of opposition from Congress, he still did a great job; he pulled the country out of a depression, when things were looking bad for America. I feel that the President has elevated the status of blacks around the world by making it to the Presidency and completing two terms".

My half-brother on my father's side, Ronnie Williams of Austin, Texas, who spent a lot of time in Arkansas and North Carolina, stated that: "I think that the president is doing a great job, on a scale of one to ten, I would give him a ten. Think about the problems in office when he took over, and I feel in my heart that he is truly working for all the people, not just blacks and Hispanics".

My daughter, Shantel M. McDaniels of Sacramento, California, a registered Nurse, mother of four beautiful children; my grandchildren, Chalena, Angelique, Imani and Dwight, are constantly reminded of the importance of a college education. Shantel believes that the first black President will have a positive impact on the civil rights struggle in America, "the president is a positive role model for black children, and black children will become motivated by his example, to reach for higher achievements in life."

My brother, Larry R. Williams of Denver, Colorado, said, "I would also give Obama a ten, because his hands were tied, he did what he had to do for the American people during bad times. Obama survived as President through a first term by meeting republicans halfway; now on a second term, the President has the freedom and support to really make a difference; he doesn't have to settle for less, or meet opposition half way."

My cousin, John Wayne Thrower of Little Rock, Arkansas stated that "people in the south just learned to live with the history that we were treated badly. We had to turn a blind eye, see no evil, speak no evil, hear no evil; there was not much we could do about racial injustice. We continue to go to church and pray for a better day, our faith in God will see us through". John said he was discriminated against many times; once he was a supervisor for the Arkansas Highway Transportation Department, he left his job for three months to live in Denver, CO. with our family for a while; but when he returned, he could not get his job back. Another white employee who worked with him got his job back after being gone for a year. On another occasion, he was next in line for a promotion in the Army National Guard; the position was given to a white guy that he trained, out of frustration he quit the guards.

My close friend, Willie Flowers of Seattle, WA, stated in 2008, "I did not want Obama to win the elections, because as President, I thought he would just get assassinated like the rest of our leaders." Willie has changed his mind lately, he recently stated that the president is doing a great job, that he had to work hard his first term because of the hand he was dealt. The president started out in a big hole, there was war, and economic collapse; but he pulled the country together. On a scale of one to ten, I give him a ten. President Obama is a perfect example of how a President should perform in office. He is not prejudiced, and has shown by example, that he works on behalf of all the American people.

Our close friend Rick Hart of Oakland, California, stated that "even when you tear down one barrier of discrimination, another pops up; now the wealthy discriminates against the poor, by developing exclusive million dollar housing communities; if you can't afford a million dollar home, you can't live in that neighbourhood. This practice does nothing for community diversity."

My close friend, O.W. Williams, of Seattle, WA, stated that you could notice the change in attitudes of white co-workers when going to work the first day after the Obama elections. "I noticed white people who usually did not talk much to black people were going out of their way to say good morning and start a conversation."

My close friend, Kerry D. Finch, of Seattle, WA; said that "not all the presidents were helpful to the prosperity of blacks. Ronald Reagan's administration cut out a lot of social programs started during the Kennedy Administration as a result of 1972 Equal Employment Act, CETA (Comprehensive Employment and Training Act), a great program for women and kids who were living in poverty, single parent homes and made it possible for women and kids to get jobs. Kids can earn money through summer jobs to pay for school books, clothes and other necessities that their parent could not afford. I was angry with the Reagan Administration, because I was one of those CETA kids."

Summary

This book was written so all humanity, in the name of God, can co-exist, understand and respect the rights of others to enjoy life, liberty and the pursuit of happiness. The comparison of growing up black in the North and South was a way of life best described through the eyes of black people living the experience.

The analogy of baseball to the black struggle has been a concept floating around in the minds of our black grandfathers since the beginning of baseball. Baseball became a way of communicating for many black men; terms like 'don't strike out', 'step up to the plate', and 'hit a home run'. Black history describes how many great black baseball players had to endure racial discrimination on and off the playing fields, they had one strike against them just because they were black. Blacks were not allowed three strikes at bat until The First Black President of America.

The days of the 'good old boys', all white male policy and rule making are coming to an end; today we have more minorities and women in higher legislative positions of authority in our local, state and federal government. Many laws that discriminate against minorities and women are slowly becoming a thing of the past; but there is still work to be done.

Strong religious backgrounds have enabled black people to endure a long history of injustices and discrimination. Faith in God and His promise of better things to come gave black people the hope and strength they so desperately needed to persevere, and look to the future.

The days of living in fear of physical violence and lynching are nearing an end in America; but we still have Stand Your Ground laws which target minorities. The fear of job security, medical coverage, comfortable life style and a decent retirement plan remains a major concern in the lives of many black families. Many studies have proven that discrimination in housing, employment, medical coverage, criminal justice and retirement systems still exist in America today.

The Separate But Equal laws of yesterday were a vehicle for discrimination used in post slavery days to justify segregation; and it still exists today, in the form of housing development and community planning. There have been numerous research studies done over the years that showed unfair housing practices are directed toward minorities. I can remember watching an evening news special s which videotaped black couples who were turned down for home loans by banks, denied property rentals by landlords just because they were black. When the researchers sent white couples, with the same financial status to those places, the loans were approved and the properties were rented.

Systematic discrimination is when a whole system directly or indirectly discriminated against certain groups of people. The housing industry can build exclusive communities, that out price low and medium income families. Most Americans can't afford to live in million dollar homes, yet we are all taxed for highway, roads and community improvements, some of this money is being used to subsidize the builders of exclusive neighbourhoods that most people can't afford.

We can level the playing field by continuing the peaceful, nonviolent efforts of Dr Martin Luther King Jr. We need to continue with employment work quotas and affirmative action. Pressure our legislators to legalize marijuana. Medical marijuana has been recommended by physicians for centuries, and is legal in Colorado, Washington and a few other countries. In ancient India and China, cannabis was used as an antiemetic, pain reliever, and for gastro intestinal disorders. Legalizing marijuana would be an economic boost for the country; profits from sales taxes and savings from the decreased criminal justice system, expenses for housing and prosecuting marijuana offenders would be huge. This would put an end to racial profiling, prevent so many young black youths from having a criminal record, being introduced to the correctional system; it would also reduce the overcrowding of our jails and prisons. We have medical documentation of the health benefits of marijuana, yet it is still classified as an illegal drug in most States. Why? Because of lobbyist for the big pharmaceutical drug, tobacco and alcohol companies who do not want free enterprise competition. The fears of special interest groups are that if people used marijuana to relieve symptoms of stress, HIV, Parkinson's, glaucoma and pain, some people would not pay the highly inflated cost of manufacturing, processing and sales of prescription drugs, alcohol and cigarettes.

We need to be proactive in addressing the issues of overcrowding of hospitals, emergency rooms and outpatient clinics, by reducing our dependency on alcohol and cigarettes, which are the direct causes of the major long term illnesses like chronic obstructive pulmonary disease, heart attacks, strokes, and liver disease. The American government should enforce strict environmental control standards, and health regulations on big manufacturing businesses. We must address the issues of pollution, global warming, and the destruction of the ozone layer which protects our planet from harmful ultra violet sun rays, and the preservation of our polar ice cap.

The state lotteries programs need to be reorganized for the purpose of a better distribute of wealth to the American people. We need to put more money into more people's hands and back into the economy. Lottery officials are making huge salaries, for what? Why don't they do their jobs, use their brains to help the economy? When the winnings get over 2 million dollars, then the winners of two and three correct numbers should get more money, what is with this $3.00 and $6.00 winner crap? Poor people throughout the states spend their hard-earned money to play the lottery, tricked by constant advertising about how you could be the next big winner, and the American dream awaits you, but you have to play to win. In a bad economy, people are vulnerable; this activity to me is predatory. Out of desperation, you play, and get 4 numbers correct, you get $40.00, which happened to me once, and then one winner gets $150 million. That is not fair to the millions of other players who are victimized by false advertisement. Why don't the lottery and casino industry try to help people with gambling addictions? Why don't they show the down side of gambling; couples having marital problems, people getting evicted because they gambled away their rent, or car payments late, show the realities of life? What do the winners do with the money? Many don't think about the world economy, or people living in poverty. Most big winners hoard their money, locked away in a private or foreign bank account while our economy goes down the drain. When those big winners die, one family member, the lawyers and the banks gets most of the money; so you have the same scenario with the rich getting richer, and the poor getting poorer. We should demand better management and distribution of big lottery winnings; I think that if you get four of six winning numbers, and the jackpot is 150 million, you should get a least 1 million, not $40.00.

We need a system of universal healthcare, millions of Americans are without healthcare coverage and a million others are without adequate coverage. This alone will tear down the walls of inequality and healthcare diversities in America. Free healthcare and human rights are inseparable moral issues; and its opponents are special interest groups; groups motivated by greed, power, and a total disrespect for the basic needs of other human beings. America, how long will we continue to allow ourselves to be held hostage to the personal profit motivated demands of big businesses, big pharmaceutical and big insurance companies? Their profit motivated greed is detrimental to the health and welfare of all Americans; why give tax breaks and incentives? The tobacco, alcohol and pharmaceutical industries should have stronger federal regulations on marketing and distributions, for the protection of public health. Insurance companies should not be allowed to increase rates for profit or deny claims for pre-existing conditions to save money. The evidence is out there, just look on the internet; most premature deaths in the United States are indirectly related to cigarette, alcohol and pharmaceutical drug consumption, and insurance companies deny most of those health related claims; most life insurance policies state that death must be of natural causes. You pay all your life into life insurance, health insurance and unemployment insurance, and when you need help, the insurance companies deny your claim, and if you can't afford a lawyer, what do you do?

If you look up stress response on Taber's Cyclopaedic Medical Dictionary, the stress response can cause physical and psychological demands on the human body, the response is slightly different between individuals, but in most people, physically, your heart beats faster, your breathing increases, blood is rerouted to major muscle groups in preparation for flight or fight. Psychologically, a person can become depressed and develop tension headaches and ulcers from stress and anxiety. I remember from nursing school that there is an increased risk of cellular damage by free radicals when the brain and heart is oxygen deprived during long periods of stress; the kind of stress many black people had to endure for over 400 years before civil rights laws were enacted, and still exist for many blacks in certain areas of the south. Stress can cause memory loss; Alzheimer's and heart problems later in life. The stress factor puts black people at a high risk for many medical conditions related to endocrine (diabetes), respiratory and cardiac problems.

In the end, God will have spoken, let there be peace and unity. We should all be proud as Americans that as a nation, there is less racism and personal phobias today than ever, we are more concerned with non-violent methods of resolving conflict, and we continue to get better. The election of a minority to the Presidency brings unity to the country, and helps eliminate negative stereotyping, and forces us to look closer at the equality and love philosophies of past leaders like Abraham Lincoln and Martin Luther King.

Our black fathers and grandfathers can be proud that we as a nation have made significant progress to even the baseball fields of America. Black people today have a voice, political and legal representation to make a difference, to appeal the unfair discriminatory laws like the Three Strikes and Stand Your Ground laws.

Finally, black people are starting to get their full three strikes at bat in America. More blacks have equal opportunity, equal protection under the law, and now we have equal representation on and off the baseball fields of life. Black people can now move forward in any profession, achieve self-actualization as a race.

Bibliography

Internet Google Search: National Health Care Disparities Report viewed 07/01/08.

The Book of Negro Folklore: Langston Hughes, 1960's.

The Seattle Stranger: weekly publication September 2008. Dominec Holden, Marijuana.

Tabor Cyclopaedic Medical Dictionary, Edition 18, F.A.Davis 1997

PBS Home Video Lincoln 1992

The Holy Bible, Revised Standard Version: Thomas Nelson & Sons, New York 1953

http://en.wikipedeia.org/wiki/New_York_Black_Yankees

http://www.nydailynews.com/sports/baseball/yankees/2009. From Internet 2009.

http://www.historyplace.com. The Dred Scott Decision; Internet 06/06/09

http://en.wikipedia.org. Plessy v. Ferguson; Internet 06/06/09

http://www.negroleaguebaseball.com/history 101; Negro Baseball League: Internet 8/26/08

http://www.npr.org. Reagan, the south and Civil Rights: 7/13/09

http://www.harbay.net/history.html.History of Hemp. Internet 5/22/10

http://www.pbs.org. Race Based Legislation in the North: 2000 Warner Home Video.

http://www.clintonpresidentialcenter.org/. Hillary Rodham Clinton: 7/14/09

http://findarticles.com/. 50 years of blacks in baseball: 7/14/09

www.presidentprofiles.com/AndrewJacksonslavery).8/26/08

http://hnn.us/articles/10827. /George Washington's Slave Child.

http://en.wikipedia.org/wiki/ThomasJefferson/Grant/Internet 2009

http://en.wikipedia.org/wiki/ Civil Rights Act of 1866

http://www.gale.cengage.com/FDR and race relations.

http://en.wikipedia.org/wiki/tuskegee/study/syphilis /Internet 2009

http://www.wikipedia.org/ Eisenhower/internet 2009

http://library.thinkquest.org/j10112391/jfk/htm.Internet 2009

http://pumpub.krose.org/forum/ Nixon's Universal Health Care. Internet 2009

http://www.presidency.ucsb.edu/ws/ Jimmy Carter Healthcare Legislation. 1977

http://www.dems.gov/ Inaugural Address William J. Clinton 1993

http://en.wikipedia.org/wiki/clinton_health_care_plan_1993) Internet 2009

http://www.presidentialtimeline.org / President Clinton, Civil Rights/Internet 2009

http://en.wikipedia.org/wiki/ Reagan/Johnson. Internet 2009

http://www.npr.org/ Templates/ Reagan, the South and Civil Rights. 2009.

http://www.encyclopedia.com/doc/1G2-2536601700. The Suffrage Movement: 1997.

http://www.nhi.org/online/issues/147/ provilidgedplaces.html: Fall 2006.

http://ethicalego.com/Relations/blog4.php/2009. Internet 2010

http://nobelprize.org The Nobel Peace Prize for 2009.Interner 2010

http://uspolitics.about.com/od/usgovernment/a/filibuster.ht m. Internet 2010